MILWAUKEE MEMORIES:

Milwaukee and Hollywood
&
Small Town Secrets

ISBN: 978-0-932270-52-8
ISBN: 0-932270-52-2

Order from:
The Spencer Press
79 Walnut Street Unit 4
Newtonville, MA. 02460-1331

(617) 965-8388
jacknusan@earthlink.net
www.drjackporter.com

977.515
P83M
2011

CONTENTS

PART TWO: SMALL TOWN SECRETS

PREFACE FOR *MILWAUKEE MEMORIES*

This was supposed to be two separate books because they were so different, but I listened to my good friend Gerry Glazer and made them into one book. The first half "Milwaukee and Hollywood" is pretty straightforward, and needs little explanation plus, it was fun to write. However, the second half "Small Town Secrets" was more difficult and like a birth, came out in its own due time, late in life, when most of the survivors had died and their children were pushing social security age.

No one else could have written this story, but I knew that the media will ignore the rest—the movies, the suicides, the sudden deaths—to focus on the concealed adoptions and other scandalous tales of the second generation of survivors. Why? Because, for so long we tried to shelter the image of the survivors— we saw them as "perfect," with no flaws, but they were not perfect and they were not perfect parents; in fact, some of them were very poor parents.

But, at our age, today, in our late 50s and 60s, we have to accept them as flawed human beings. We need to forgive them and ourselves. They did the best they could with their limited parental skills during the hard adaptation to this new country.

They made mistakes. Who should we blame? Hitler? The Nazis? Their suffering? Their losses? It really does not matter anymore. It is what it is and it was what it was. Let us not inflict on our own children and grandchildren what our parents inflicted, knowingly or unknowingly, upon us.

It is time to forgive and move on. Rabbi Nachman of Bratslav has a great parable of what we must do: He wrote that life is a narrow, treacherous bridge, posed between two mountains—one mountain is birth and the other is death. Our task, my friends, is to walk that narrow bridge and not be afraid.

Let us not be afraid.

Dr. Jack Nusan Porter
Newtonville, Mass.
jacknusan@earthlink.net
August 18, 2011

PART ONE

MILWAUKEE & HOLLYWOOD

Dedication

Dedicated to James Auer
of the *Milwaukee Journal-Sentinel*,
mentor, friend, and guru of everything Hollywood
and more. I miss him greatly.

ACKNOWLEDGMENTS

First and foremost, I owe a tremendous debt to Jim Auer, to whom I dedicated this long overdue book. It was a tragedy that Jim died so suddenly and so young. I really needed his support and wisdom. Without that support at the beginning, this book would have been less complete.

Thanks also to Stephanie Boris of the Pacific Film Archives; to the Wisconsin and Milwaukee Historical Societies (for photos and leads); to Jay Hyland and Kathy Bernstein of the Milwaukee Jewish Museum for photos and leads; to Adam Pertman for his knowledge of adoptions; and to the late Charlotte Zucker (mother of Jerry and David Zuker), Gene Wilder (a momentary meeting at a book signing in Boston. Thank you, Mr. Wilder); to David Zucker (a brief note); and to childhood friends such as Joey Blasberg, Hershel Weingrod, and Stu Chapman. I even found out that a Mirisch Brother granddaughter attended UW-Madison. Gerry Glazer, Sheldon Bankier and Arnie Peltz also provided me with some insights. I also thanks to my cousin Allen Porter who never forgot his connection to LA. Thank you to all and apologies if I forgot someone.

INTRODUCTION

There has always been this mysterious, inexplicable relationship between Milwaukee and Hollywood, going back a hundred years. Wisconsinites, especially those from Jewish backgrounds, have been a part of Hollywood since its very beginnings. In short, why and how did one county, in fact, four high schools in that county (Washington, Shorewood, Nicolet, and Whitefish Bay High) produce so many Hollywood-bound producers, directors, actors, and screenwriters?

It seems that Milwaukee (in some strange way) was there at the beginning. People from Milwaukee were involved in every single epoch of Hollywood from the early days to the present. And not just Milwaukee, but all of Wisconsin contributed.

Why? I have pondered this question for decades, especially since several childhood friends went out to California in the 1970's and became part of that world.

Is it because the Midwest epitomizes the "essential American," that is, what the world thinks of when we say "American" is the Midwestern American? Its accent is the "neutral" American accent, since the Midwest is the very center of America, and Milwaukee is the very center of the Midwest and so, Milwaukee, Wisconsin reflects the quintessential American values of wholesome goodness, friendliness, and uprightness. Maybe. Or was it because California enticed people as a place to start a new life, to throw off the old burdens? Or was it simply the weather? I know my Uncle Morris and Aunt Betty and their son Allen, went west for health and weather reasons—Betty's health and the Chicago winters were not fun any more. It's the same reason New Englanders and New Yorkers (that includes you Jersey guys and gals as well) go to Florida. In fact, data from the 100th anniversary of Washington High School (WHS) in Milwaukee showed that the largest number of alumni outside of Wisconsin lived in California and Florida.

American Jews were trying to prove their allegiance to their beloved country, and what better way than in movies? If we look at Jews in Hollywood in general, from the very beginning, we see an insecure group of immigrants latching onto a new industry with tremendous growth potential, an industry ignored for the most part by mainstream non-Jews (John F. Kennedy's father was an exception). Jews were always attracted to new, dangerous, and risky ventures, and they latched onto movies and made them a huge success.

It's no surprise that the early Hollywood titans were Jewish—the Lasky's, the Warner Brothers, Sam Goldwyn, Louis B. Mayer, Adolph Zukor. To this very day, Jews dominate the industry; in fact there are several anecdotes to show that even non-Jews try to pass as "Jews". In the movie *A Mighty Wind* directed by Christopher Guest (despite the name—Jewish) there

6

is a hilarious scene where a Swedish, blond, Aryan-looking producer played by a Swedish-American actor, impresses possible financial backers with his Yiddishisms just to prove how "Jewish" he is.

And even if you're Jewish, you want to be related to even more famous Jews. Jerry Zucker is a card-carrying member of the third generation of Hollywood directors and producers (the above were the first generation; the Mirisch Brothers were the second; and the Zucker-Abraham team and Steven Spielberg are the third generation); the Coen brothers are the fourth generation; and there is now a fifth generation of even younger directors and writers).

Mr. Zucker tells the story that when he first came to Hollywood, people thought he was Adolph Zukor's son; though a slightly different spelling, it sounded the same; and he did not deny the connection. Daryl Zanuck, head of 20th Century Fox, had a Jewish name but he was not Jewish. He didn't mind at all if people thought so. Compare that to a non-Jew in Boston or New York's banking or insurance business. Would he take it as a compliment if he looked Jewish or had a Jewish name? Never.

Milwaukee Memories

WHY?
SOCIOLOGICAL & HISTORICAL ISSUES

Sociologically speaking, Milwaukee Jews turned toward Hollywood for a wide range of interesting reasons. First, immigration.

Following World War II came the massive migration from the north to the south and west; my own uncle, aunt, and cousin were among them. Deborah Dash Moore in her fascinating book *To the Golden Cities: Pursuing the American Dream in Miami and L.A.* mentions some Milwaukeeans that emigrated out there. The exodus was mostly young couples in business or professions like law, medicine, and accounting, but they also included people wanting to work in Hollywood. This is backed up by data from the Washington High School alumni data bank.

In fact, I found that over 100 actors, directors, writers, and producers came out of Milwaukee (and 200 out of Wisconsin), a huge number given that Milwaukee is a smallish town compared to Chicago or New York. If we talk about Jewish people, the disproportionality is even greater. Jews make up only 2.5 percent of the Milwaukee metropolitan area population (or about 25,000 out of one million people) yet their impact on Hollywood is much higher. Hollywood is a "Jewish town," and Milwaukee contributed greatly to it.

As noted, Hollywood was a business founded by Jewish immigrants—from Carl Laemmle to Sam Goldwyn to Mayer to Fox, and onto to the Mirisch brothers, Weinstein brothers, Steven Spielberg, and others today. If we talk only of Milwaukeeans who made it in Hollywood, we would have to include the Jerry and David Zucker/Jim Abrahams team of directors, actors Gene Wilder and Charlotte Rae as well as such screen writers as Herschel Weingrod (*Trading Places, Kindergarten Cop*, and *Twins*), Joey Blasberg (*Family of Cops*), and Stu Chapman (Disney Studios). The last three I grew up with on Milwaukee's west side.

For an excellent overview of Milwaukee's contribution to movies and entertainment, see Ruth Traxler's book (1994: 52-54) which covers everyone from Harry Houdini (Harry Weiss) from Appleton to David and Jerry Zucker/Jim Abrahams (as well as Dick Chudnow) to Charlotte Rae to Gene Wilder (nee Jerry Silberman) to Jerry Hiken to Chip Zien to Herschel Weingrod to Cy Howard and onto Jackie Mason.

HAPPY DAYS REVISITED

And it was not just in film but in television too, that Milwaukeeans made a mark. It should not be a surprise, given my premise of this "wholesomeness," that such iconic TV series as "Laverne and Shirley" and "Happy Days" were all based on Milwaukee characters and locations. Even a spinoff, "Mork and Mindy," took place in Milwaukee.

The characters were created by Milwaukeean Tom Miller. In Miller's "Happy Days" series, Arnold's Drive-In is based on the Milky Way, now Kopps, a popular Glendale drive-in. Petroffs and Leon's were other famous drive-ins. Shotz Beer where Laverne and Shirley worked, was a combination of Blatz and Schlitz beer. The writer for the show had worked at Kopps on the east side. It exists to this day sans the drive-in car slots, the order phones that rested on your door, and the cute girls on roller skates. Miller created other TV sitcoms like "Full House" and his movies include *Silver Streak* (with Gene Wilder), *Foul Play*, and *The Best Little Whorehouse in Texas*.

My movieland "guru" Jim Auer (on right) with George Gay of Jewish Family Service and me - 1970's.

THE GENERATIONS OF MOVIE MAKERS:

THE EARLY YEARS

Carl Laemmle (1867-1939) was the founder of Universal Pictures in 1912. He was from Milwaukee. The Aitken Brothers, especially Harry Aitken, were from Milwaukee. Their business, Epoch Pictures/Triangle Pictures, built the studios where MGM's Tom Ince and Culver City Studios' D.W. Griffith made *Birth of a Nation* and *Intolerance*.

THE WAR YEARS: 1939-1945

Surprisingly, Hollywood was afraid to touch the Holocaust; World War II they could handle in their famous *Why We Fight* series; it even made movies about Nazi spies and later about anti-Semitism and racism, even disability prejudice (*Gentleman's Agreement, Crossfire, Pinky, The Best of Everything*). Interestingly, sociological studies showed that anti-Semitism went up during the War but declined afterwards. Why? Jewish, Black and other minorities like Italians returned to their hometowns and big cities demanding a bigger slice of the pie and to be treated with respect. The War tossed together people of different classes, regions, races, religions, and creeds. You couldn't exactly tell your fellow GI, the one you braved death with in the trenches of Okinawa or the beaches of Normandy, that he could not work with or live with you or join your club or stay at your hotel. Thus, barriers fell quickly for white minorities like Jews or Italians; blacks, the disabled, Native Americans, Latinos, and gays would take a little longer; but eventually all the barriers fell, at least in public transportation, housing, school, and even jobs.

It's also ironic to note that in the late 1970s, when my sister Bella and I made the rounds of Hollywood with my "partisans" script in hand to convince them to make a movie about Jewish resistance during the Shoah; we were met with either silence or strange requests.

I remember one producer asking me, after hearing our pitch about our parent's life in the forests of northwestern Ukraine as Soviet partisans: "Where's the sex?" I said, "this is the Holocaust; this is my mother we're talking about—what does sex have to do with it?' He said "We have to have sex or action every ten minutes or else the audience will fall sleep!"

I think that the real reason why we didn't have a truly sympathetic Shoah movie until 1993's *Schindler's List*,—and that movie had only a hint of sex—was that the Shoah was "too Jewish" and too "powerful" for sensitive gentiles. But Hollywood had misunderstood America; or I should say that the Jewish movie makers had misunderstood America. When finally in 2009, a movie was made about Soviet Jewish partisans, called *Defiance*, it flopped at the box office because it had no sex, not even one kiss, and the action was mediocre...

14

or maybe, Jews fighting in the forests really is....boring. No jokes. No Seinfeld. No Jon Steward.

Inglorious Basterds, Quentin Tarantino's bizarre take on the Shoah, had better action and sex than *Defiance* (plus Brad Pitt) and did a bit better box office. Maybe that old producer was right. Tits and ass. That's what people want.

Yet important movies were made before the USA entered the War—*Confessions of a Nazi Spy* (1939) and *The Mortal Storm* (1940). During the War, nothing. Jewish movie producers were loath to call attention to themselves, especially with anti-Semites like Joe Kennedy warning them, "This will be seen as *your* war."

According to Ty Burr (2008), the Holocaust was rarely treated directly on American screens until the late 50s and early 60s with the re-release of *The Juggler* starring Kirk Douglas, *The Diary of Anne Frank*, and *Judgment at Nuremberg*. A lesser-known film was Sam Fuller's 1959 B movie *Verboten*; one of the first to incorporate newsreel footage of Nazi atrocities.

Hollywood matured with the 1993 *Schindler's List* and later with Roman Polanski's 2002 *The Pianist* and Tim Blake Nelson's *The Grey Zone*, but Polanski is basically a European, not an American, and Tim Blake is an oddity cult figure. By and large, Americans were uneasy about making Shoah films. Yet still, Jewish 'resistance" films did appear in the 2000's—Robert Zwick's *Defiance* starring Daniel Craig and Quentin Tarantino's *Inglorious Basterds* with Brad Pitt.

Defiance has a neat tie-in with my own work. In 2008, Boston-based producer Steve Samuels called me and said he had a film script that he wanted to show me. I rushed over and saw the script for Nechama

15

Tec's *Defiance* book based on the Bielski Brother's *otryad* (Soviet fighting force) which saved 1,200 Jewish lives. He asked me if he should produce it. I said "Of course, Steve. I'm sorry it's not my parents' story which was similar, but yes, we need such movies that show that not all Jews went like the proverbial sheep to slaughter." He said he was interested but that Zwick needed $20 million, and that was a little too rich for Steve at the time. A good decision, since the real estate market, Steve's business, plummeted within the year.

The movie however was made, but flopped at the box office for the reasons I puckishly noted above: not enough sex and not enough real action. Or maybe that Jews are kind of boring at the box office unless funny. Nobody can identify with fighting Jews except the Israeli army and they ain't too popular anymore. You couldn't make an *Exodus*, for example, today. Nobody would buy it.

Only the Europeans make good Shoah movies… starting with *Night and Fog* and continuing on to a dozen great films such as *Europa, Europa* and *The Pianist*. American directors are incapable of making good Shoah movies.

My introduction to Hollywood and the War came in the late 1950s when I came across a book that tantalized me greatly. It was a fabulous collection of photos and commentary in the famous *Look* magazine style and was called *Movie Lot to Beachhead: The Motion Picture Goes to War and Prepares for the Future* by the editors of *Look*, with a preface by Robert St. John. While it hardly mentioned Jews and the Holocaust, it was powerful and haunting, and its pictures stayed with me forever. It was a continuation of my love affair with Hollywood, with the power of moving pictures in the aid of war, propaganda, or education. And of course, there were actors from Milwaukee and Wisconsin like Spencer Tracy who made a contribution to the war effort.

Jews played an important role in the war as well, Milwaukee Jews no less than anyone else.

I watched a lot of movies in the 50s and kept a lot of "lists." Why, I don't know. Maybe it was the beginning of teaching myself "research"—I had a Spiral "Sight Saver" Stenographer's Note Book from around 1956, which would make me eleven years old, and it had lists like "sites in Milwaukee" (parks, hotels, public buildings), books in my collection, the number of baseball cards and coins I had, types of cigarettes, movies seen "since July 7th, 1956" and movie theaters "seen" or "been in."

I am glad I made such a list—since many of these movies are long forgotten (yet quite a few are legendary) and about eighty percent of the movie theaters have been demolished like the Uptown near 51ˢᵗ and North Avenue (mentioned in Gene Wilder's memoir) or vacant (like the Sherman at 48ᵗʰ and Burleigh).

The movies I listed in 1956 were *The Revolt of Mamie Stover, Santiago, Safaria (sic), Crime in the Streets, Toy Tiger, Bhowani Junction, Song of the South, Trapeze, Johnny Concho, Moby Dick, The Maverick Queen, Pardners (sic), Congo Crossing, Notorious, Cheaper by the Dozen, The African Lion, War and Peace, Girl on the Red Velvet Swing, Unguarded Moment, Tension at Table Rock, King and I, Sharkfighters, Back from Eternity* (interest-

17

ingly, not *From Here to Eternity*), *High Noon, 7th Cavalry, The Mole People, Everything but the Truth, Curucu: Monster of the Jungle, Untamed Women, Savage Princess, Hollywood or Bust, The Iron Petticoat,* and *Fear Strikes Out.*

Thirty-three films in all, some of them seem a bit "R"-rated for an eleven-year old. This was the golden age of movies, and the theaters were often either extravagant or simple neighborhood hideouts. The ones I actually went into included the Uptown, Sherman, Riverside, Roosevelt, Towne, Savoy, Fox-Bay, Alhambra, and Milwaukee; others that I simply saw from the outside were the Palace, Warner, Wisconsin, Ogden, Franklin, Strand, Oriental, Varsity, Telenews, Princess, Kino (a German language theater), Peerless, Downer, and Paradise. Of course, as I grew older and wiser, I went downtown and went into some of the latter, especially for big block busters like *The Sound of Music* or sleazy R-rated films (before there were ratings) shown at the Princess or Paradise, which showed art house films with semi-naked women and adult themes. At one time, the movie *Marty* was considered an art house "adult" film that my friends and I had to sneak into.

Out of twenty-three theaters, only about six or seven still exist: the luxurious Oriental and art houses like the Downer or neighborhood ones like the Fox-Bay, plus one or two downtown. (For a full panoply of these wonderful theaters, see the book *Silver Screens* by Larry Widen and Judi Anderson).

The movies on Saturday July 19, 1958 in MIlwaukee

THE SECOND GENERATION: THE 40's AND 50's

The Mirisch Brothers form the second generation of producers. Harold J. Mirisch (1907-1997)
was a film buyer for Warner theaters in Wisconsin
from 1930-1937; zone manager from 1937-1941, and
exhibitor in Milwaukee from 1941-1946 for RKO
among other studios. He was later vice-president of
Monogram Pictures and Allied Artists in 1947 and
later, in 1957, he became president of the Mirisch
Company.

His younger brother by fourteen years, Walter M.
Mirisch (1921-) came to Milwaukee and Madison
from New York City in the late 1930's and graduated
the University of Wisconsin–Madison in 1943. Walter
was Vice-President of Mirisch Company in the 1950s
and in 1960-1961, president of the Screen Producers Guild and a member of the Board of Governors
of the Academy of Motion Picture Arts and Sciences
(AMPAS) that distributes the Oscars, and its Vice-
President from 1969-1972.

A third brother was Marvin Mirisch (1918-2002).
Walter Mirisch and his brothers have close ties to
UW–Madison; their grandchildren have gone there.

They produced such classics as *West Side Story*, *Some
Like it Hot*, and *Irma La Douce* with Jack Lemmon as
well the Doris Day-Rock Hudson comedies like *Pillow
Talk*. plus *By Love Possessed*, *Two for the Seesaw*, *Toys in
the Attic*, and the Academy Award-winning film *In the
Heat of the Night* with Rod Stieger and Sidney Poitier.

It's also possible they were connected as producers
and distributors to a little-known Humphrey Bog-
art cult film called *Two Guys from Milwaukee*. It was
directed by David Butler who had done *The Road*

to *Morocco*, *My Wild Irish Rose*, and *Tea for Two*. The screenplay for *Two Guys* was done by the talented I.A. L. Diamond, who had worked with Billy Wilder as writer for *The Apartment* with Jack Lemmon and Shirley Maclaine, and *Some Like it Hot* with Marilyn Monroe, Tony Curtis, Joe. E. Brown and the ubiquitous Jack Lemmon.

Pat O'Brien, also from Milwaukee, often played the Irish cop or priest and was a friend of Spencer Tracy. He played the title role in *Knute Rockne, All American* and the Irish detective in *Some Like it Hot*.

Robert Bloch, a novelist and screenwriter, is on the cusp of these two generations. His most famous movie was *Psycho* (1960), directed by Alfred Hitchcock. His novel upon which the film is based was inspired by a real-life story of serial killer Ed Gein, who was also the model for *The Texas Chainsaw Massacre* and *Silence*

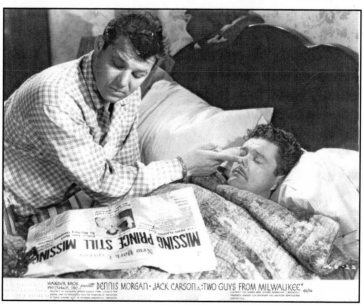

Publicity picture for "Two Guys from MIlwaukee, 1946

of the Lambs. For those of you wish to forget, Gein… was known for luring and killing elderly ladies, and using their skin and body parts for lampshades and other stuff. He kept the bodies around similar to Jeffrey Dahmer (though Gein was from the small town of Plainfield and Jeffrey Dahmer was from Milwaukee). The embalmed "mother" in *Psycho* echoes this as does the skin souvenirs from *Silence of the Lambs*. Gein died in prison; and Dahmer was killed in prison.

Why does Milwaukee always get a bum rap? With Ed Gein and Dahmer, you'd think that Milwaukee and Wisconsin were swarming with zombie-like psychos, yet juxtaposed with this image is the sweet and innocent "Happy Days"—Laverne and Shirley—Mork and Mindy image. What gives? It's a mystery how one city can echo these two diverse images.

Personal note: I never saw or met either one, thank God, but I did visit Gein's house and I almost tried to see Dahmer in prison, but did see his apartment building near Marquette University. Thankfully both have been torn down or else weirdoes (including this author) would have picked up a brick or a piece of wood as a memento. They are still eerie to see, even the location of the old farm house in Plainfield, especially at dusk. I don't recommend it. Stay away. The ghost of Ed Gein lives.

Second personal note: As a criminology teacher at Bridgewater State College in Massachusetts in the 1990s I took my class to Bridgewater State Hospital and we saw the notorious child killer Edward Meinhof. I said hello to him as he walked by—true story—and the guard admonished me not to speak to the prisoner-patient. Surprisingly, one can take one's sociology and criminology classes to tour state hospitals while the patients are walking about, but you can't talk to them. There was however never any danger from them. But it is still the closest I have ever come to a serial killer.

However, there was another side to the 1950's—a darker, more complex side—of subdued violence, drug addictions, McCarthyite paranoia, racism, and especially the "secret side" of fame and money—where even "super heroes" kill themselves.

One film that reflected those times and has always intrigued me was *Hollywoodland*, a 2005 film starring Ben Affleck, Diane Lane, Adrian Brody, and Bob Hoskins. It is the story of the life and death of "Superman", George Reeves. What is so intriguing about the film that it evokes not only my hero Superman but also the LA that I knew as a child in the 50's. My folks made several trips to LA by train, on the California Zephyr or the Southwest Chief, to visit our Uncle Morris and Aunt Betty as well as cousin Allen—Betty and Morris's child; and later my Uncle Boris and Aunt Hinda and their children—Sam, Jack, and Abe.

One of the scenes in that movie takes place in a small house on South Curson, near Fairfax and Pico, one very similar to the one Boris and Hinda lived in, with its huge palm tree in front and its lemon and lime trees in back in their tiny backyard. It was just like their house. Second, the Toni Mannix character, Superman's lover, reminded me of my Aunt Betty—a beautiful but manipulative woman, plus the entire feel and look of the film echoed my memories of Hollywood in the 50's. When Superman "killed" himself, it was the first shock to many of us youngsters. The second was the TV quiz show scandals with Charles Van Doren, and the last was the death of JFK. That sealed it. After that, we lost our innocence; we were no longer children.

THE CRAZY 60's AND 70's GENERATION

A great many of my friends went west in the 60's and 70's right after college. They packed their bags and went to either LA or San Francisco. Why? For the same reasons mentioned above: a new life, sunny weather, an exciting career, maybe politics, maybe Hollywood. Several became screenwriters: Joey Blasberg, Herschel Weingrod, and Stu Chapman. Most of them I never heard from again after they left. I always had to go out there to see them; they never came to Boston to see me.

Joey (now called Joel) Blasberg was most well-known for his *Family of Cops* series of films, starring Charles Bronson, but he was involved with others, including a documentary on the withdrawal from Gaza, with childhood friend, Arnie Peltz.

Weingrod's most famous movie was the screenplay he co-wrote with Timothy Harris for the 1983 Paramount film *Trading Places* with Eddie Murphy and Dan Aykroyd with star turns by such ancient and venerable actors as Don Ameche (from Wisconsin), Ralph Bellamy, and Denholm Elliott.

Stu Chapman wrote for the Disney Company.

Bob Uecker and Chip Zien and—even *Playboy*'s Miss April 1970 (Barbara Hillary)—were all from Milwaukee.

I knew Mickey Marcus from the old Jewish Center on Prospect Ave. He was a well-known local actor who went out to Hollywood and starred in a few roles.

However the most famous of the all Milwaukeeans to go out to Hollywood as directors were the Zucker Brothers/Abraham team.

THE ZUCKER BROTHERS/ABRAHAM TEAM

Jerry and David Zucker and their late mother Charlotte, who appeared in all their movies, were all from Milwaukee. Trivia: The last movie that O.J. Simpson appeared in was a Zucker brother's movie called *The Naked Gun* (1989) with Leslie Nielsen and Elvis Presley's wife, Priscilla. The team also used many Milwaukee allusions in their movies—Galena Street, for example—even if only 70 people found the joke funny.

Entertainment Weekly named *Airplane* (1980) 67th on a list of the 100 Greatest Movies of all time, a surprise choice ahead of *M* with Peter Lorre, *Potemkin*, and *The Best Years of Our Lives*. (*Psycho* written by a Milwaukeean was 11th, the highest ranking "Milwaukee" film on the list). One could say a lot more about this team and their beginnings in Milwaukee and in Madison, starting with their classic cult film *Kentucky Fried Movie*, directed by John Landis. The film had its origins at the University of Wisconsin in Madison as a theatrical production. The Zucker brothers, and their friends, Jim Abraham and Dick Chudnow, all started out in Milwaukee and went out to Hollywood, but Chudnow returned to Milwaukee and later founded "ComedySportz," an organized competition among improvisational comedians and comedy teams.

But, arguably the most famous actor to come out of Milwaukee in modern times was Gene Wilder (though Spencer Tracy is right up there at the top as well).

GENE WILDER

Gene Wilder started life as Jerome (Jerry) Silberman, Washington High School (WHS), Class of 1953. He went to my high school; but he's a decade older than me. There are still many people who remember him. He left Milwaukee at a young age, first as a stage actor in New York, and then to Hollywood. His most famous collaborations were with Mel Brooks in such classics as *Blazing Saddles*, *Young Frankenstein* (Fran-ken-steen!), and especially *The Producers*, plus, *Willy Wonka and the Chocolate Factory*. Later he made a series of hilarious "Black-Jewish' films with Richard Pryor— For example, *See No Evil, Hear No Evil*.

Entertainment Weekly named *The Producers* (1968) the 88th on its list of the 100 greatest movies of all time. *Willy Wonka and the Chocolate Factory* is, however, his most iconic film.

He married comedienne Gilda Radner but when she died, something in him also "died" and he left Hollywood. Today, he is happily remarried, living near Bridgeport, Connecticut, and writing romantic novels and lovely memoirs such as *Kiss Me Like a Stranger*.

After many tries, I met him and talked to him briefly at a Barnes and Noble reading and signing in downtown Boston. I also met his lovely wife. "Hello, I'm Jack Porter from Washington High School, and here is a yearbook from that time (1961-62)."

26

He was a bit startled and taken aback, but said "So happy to meet you."

After the signing I asked his wife if she would ask Gene if I could come visit him and interview him for this book; she discussed it with him and sadly came over to me and said: "Gene is sorry but he doesn't wish to, but it was lovely to ask." She herself seemed sadly disappointed as if she wanted to know more about his Milwaukee life.

But it is an open book. He has family in Milwaukee (plus a sister in New York City) and many WHS class-

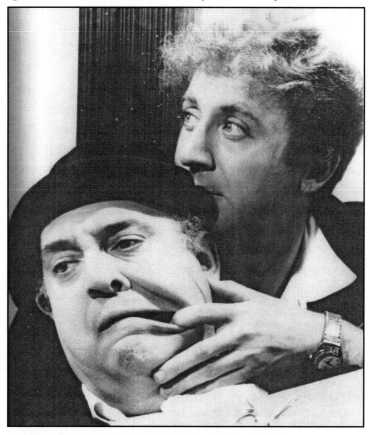

Gene Wilder & Zero Mostel from The Producers, 1967

mates still remember him—especially the class of '53. Interestingly, he was overshadowed in high school by a more adventurous guy, but not as successful actor and director—Tom Laughlin.

TOM LAUGHLIN

His most famous role was as Billy Jack. I've interviewed people who knew him and the image that comes to mind is like that motorcycle-driving, poetry-writing, dark haired good looking guy in *Peggy Sue Got Married* whom Peggy Sue falls in love with. McLaughlin had that same rep in high school in the early 50's—a beautiful girlfriend, girls swooning at his good looks and sexy posture. He still brings back dreamy memories from septugarians I talked to.

Billy Jack is a cult movie today. It's about what Tom Laughlin was—a motorbikin' outlaw in the mold of James Dean and Marlon Brando, a "rebel without a cause" common in the mid-50's, the ultimate "greaser," so-called because they used greasy pomade to keep their duck-feathered jet black or blond hair in line. Along with their black leather jackets, blue jeans, a cigarette box rolled into their clean white T-shirt, they were depicted as the tough but good-natured guys who probably ended up either in jail, dead in a car crash, or in Vietnam ten years later.

You can see such types depicted in *American Graffiti* and in *Grease* and earlier in *West Side Story*. I met several of them, and I was their Richard Dreyfus, the semi-cool smart kid, headed for college but respected for his brains and his ability to be of some use to the greasers and their girlfriends, and they always had the hottest babes.

The guy I remember most was Tony, an Italian of course, who lived across the alley from me. A really nice guy. Even had a brother with Down's syndrome that he lovingly protected. I never knew what happened to Tony. Maybe he became a plumber or a construction worker and moved to the suburbs. Never saw him again. There were many "Tony's" in my high school—some were blond like in *Grease*; some were dark like Travolta.

If you look in my WHS yearbook, you'll see a lot of guys who looked like greasers—Phil Plotkin, Kevin Landry, and Richard Parker.

They just don't make 'em like that anymore.

CHARLOTTE RAE

If I seem like I am overlooking the ladies, I apologize. But Charlotte Rae was a big star in her day. Her original name was Charlotte Rae Lubotsky, a very well-known name in Milwaukee via her mother Esther and her father—Meyer Lubotsky's Tire Sales, on 12ᵗʰ and Vliet. Her dad's ads were among the very first TV ads in the city and made him very rich and famous. And she was another WHS alumna.

Charlotte Rae was most famous for her role in the TV series *The Facts of Life* (which recently had a reunion of its stars). She also appeared in many iconic TV shows: as Sylvia Schnauzer in "Car 54, Where Are You?" ; as the eccentric Mrs. Bellotti in the 1975-76 "Hot l Baltimore"; and as the funny live-in housekeeper Mrs. Garrett in the 1977-78 "Diff'rent Strokes," the show that made eleven-year-old Gary Coleman a star. She was a very wise and funny lady, somewhat akin to an earlier Mrs. Goldberg, also Jewish and also an early TV star on "The Goldbergs." Television was less shy then about portraying Jews openly; that would change in the mid-50s after Mc-Carthyism and anti-Communism was linked to Jews, and Jewish producers were reluctant to give Jews a high profile. This was especially true after the Rosenberg's were electrocuted in 1953 for being "atomic spies" for Russia.

A good example of genteel anti-Semitism, often carried by Jews themselves, is the 1985 Robert Redford film *Quiz Show*, where the Jewish schlemiel from the Bronx Herbert Stempel (played brilliantly by John Turturro) is told to take a dive for Brahmin Ivy-League WASP intellectual Charles Van Doren (portrayed by Ralph Fiennes; and his father Mark Van Doren by Paul Schofield—two British actors). But it wasn't only that. It was shown that Jewish contestants were quickly replaced by goyish contestants, because how could America identify with nerdy shmos like Stempel and their whining wives? Scandal only changed the format. TV did not collapse; it simply swallowed up the Congressional hearings live and turned them into rating games. A very young Richard Goodwin, portrayed by Rob Morrow in the movie, saw Washington corruption and payoffs early on and tried to change things later under President John F. Kennedy and his brother, Attorney General Robert Kennedy, but with limited success.

Thus, the Jewishness was rubbed out of characters that Charlotte Rae and others would portray, and on shows like "Happy Days" and "Laverne and Shirley," there were no ostensibly Jewish characters. Ironically, however, the actor who portrayed the "Fonz," Fonza-relli, Henry Winkler, is Jewish. Richie Cunningham, Potsie, and the rest were all "American" teenagers of no particular ethnic description. This was also true of such Hollywood movies as *American Graffiti*. No discernible ethnicity is cognizant even though the role portrayed by Richard Dreyfuss, who seems a bit out of place in the movie, is probably Jewish. (There is a statue to the "Fonz" in downtown Milwaukee, by the way.)

Ever since Jackie Mason flopped as a "rabbi" in his ill-fated TV series, we have seen very few Jewish characters on TV. I know. I tried interesting Hollywood in a TV series called "Key West Rabbi"—and it sunk faster than a lead weight. However, over time, Jews became more relaxed as Americans, and we were able to see shows like "Seinfeld" as well as later shows such as "Curb Your Enthusiasm" (with Larry David, co-creator of "Seinfeld") and "Entourage." One could also add Jerry Stiller and his son Ben in movies. Both "Curb Your Enthusiasm" and "Entourage." of course, have not so lovable Jewish characters but they are still Jewish. Still later, "The Jon Stewart Show" and "The Colbert Report" openly make fun of Jewish characters and situations. There is, thank God, a new tolerance for ethnicity, and it is ethnicity, not religion, that is portrayed. The media is still wary of portraying Jews as religious people or even dealing with Judaism as a serious religion. As a cultural form, fine, but not as a religion. Of course this is also true regarding Islam and Catholicism. Stick to the stereotypes but not "too" stereotypical….and please be gentle or you'll end up like Salman Rushdie.

Sex, politics, and religion are the three most sensitive issues in America, and the ones we all love to talk about and yet all three are portrayed so badly on TV and in the movies.

The Fourth Generation & Beyond

The Coen Brothers epitomize this fourth generation. They are, of course, Jewish (probably "Cohen") and they are from the Minnesota counterpart of Milwaukee—St. Louis Park, a suburb of Minneapolis. St. Louis Park is home to not only my sister Bella Porter-Smith and her husband Mitch and their five children (Sruli, Avi, Aryeh, Shragi, and Mindy) but also several very well-known personalities: first, of course, the Coen Brothers—Ethan and Joel; plus the *New York Times* columnist and author Thomas L. Friedman and the "Saturday Night Live" writer, humorist and surprisingly, US Senator, Al Franken. All hail from this small suburb.

In fact, in the Coen Brothers film *A Serious Man* they portray their hometown but film it elsewhere in Minnesota, One scene of which I am familiar is of the synagogue, just across the street where my mother used to live for fifteen years— I spoke in that very hall, in that very sanctuary, where the bar mitzvah was filmed.

Oprah Winfrey, arguably the most successful black woman in American history, lived in Milwaukee briefly, even if her tenure there was not always pleasant according to the scandal sheets. Oprah came out of poverty and violent streets. In Kitty Kelley's unauthorized biography, there is a photo of Oprah with

33

the caption that she lived on "North Center Street".
If she indeed lived on Center Street, there is no such
place as "North" Center Street. There are only East
and West Center Street and Oprah probably lived
on West Center Street. This was not Beverly Hills. I
don't recommend walking around there late at night,
especially on the side streets.

Amy Pietz (from *Aliens in America*) is from Milwaukee.

Eric Benet is from Milwaukee.

Jessica Banks, a beautiful young lady, director, and
actress, makes up the fifth generation; and they keep
getting younger and younger, especially in Hollywood, where youth reigns supreme.

THE REST OF WISCONSIN

Milwaukee has produced many Hollywood people
but not only Milwaukee—Appleton for example produced the strange combination of Edna Ferber, Harry
Houdini, Joe McCarthy, and Willem Dafoe.

Edna Ferber, formerly a novelist, also wrote such
movies as *Cimarron*, *Showboat*, and *Dinner at Eight*.

Harry Houdini was originally Erich Weiss from Bu-
dapest. His dad was a rabbi. His brother Theo and he
went into show biz instead of the rabbinate. Similar
to Jackie Mason (nee Maza), who hailed from Sheboygan.

Joe McCarthy was in "show biz" in a way—a TV
personality who went after Commies in the State
department. He felt that Hollywood was controlled
by the Communist Party, which was a code word for
"Jewish controlled." He influenced conservative movie moguls like Louis B. Mayer and Harry Warner to

become anti-left, and that led to the "blacklist."

And Willem Dafoe, a non-Jew, has been in such Academy-award wining movies as *Platoon* and *Jesus Christ*.

Fred McMurray (1908-1991) grew up in Beaver Dam. His best films were the 40's noir *Double Indemnity* and the 50's *Son of Flubber*. Later he played the father in the TV series: "My Three Sons."

Frederic March (1897-1975), born Ernest Frederick McIntyre Bickel, was from Racine, a lovely town just a few miles south of Milwaukee and also attended the University of Wisconsin. He often played the debonair leading man. He won Oscars for *Dr. Jekyll and Mr. Hyde* and *The Best Years of Our Lives*. His other films include *A Star is Born*, *Nothing Sacred*, and *Anna Karenina*. The theater at UW–Oshkosh is named after him. He is buried on his former estate in New Milford, Conn. He was also a close friend of Spencer Tracy, and they both were in the classic film *Inherit the Wind*.

Nicholas Ray was from La Crosse. He was a 50's cult director whose films included *Rebel Without a Cause* with James Dean, Natalie Wood, and Dennis Hopper; *They Live by Night*, *Johnny Guitar*, and *Bigger Than Life*. He went to the same high school as Joseph Losey, another important "cult" director of the 50's and 60's. I met Ray once in 1969 in Chicago during the famous Chicago Seven trial, where he was making a movie on the trial, a movie that was never completed. He wore a dark eye patch and was quite the showman.

Less well-known Hollywood people included Jerry Bock (1929-2010) composer of *Fiddler on the Roof*,

Fiorello, and *Mr. Wonderful* who went to the University of Wisconsin in Madison; and Daniel J. Travanti, the captain on "Hill Street Blues," who hails from Racine.

Jackie Mason, the comic, who was in a few minor movies (*The Stoolie*) and a flop TV series was born Yankel Maza in Sheboygan, Wisconsin in 1932. He tries to hide this fact since most people think he is the ultimate New "Yawker." His father Eli Maza was a rabbi and he has a brother who is also a rabbi, Bernie Maza.

And finally, Spencer Tracy, the greatest actor to come from Wisconsin, and with the most Oscar © nominations in history—nine. Tracy (1900-1967) was born in Milwaukee and attended six high schools, including Wauwatosa East in 1915, St. John's Cathedral High for boys in 1916, Marquette Academy and West Division (now Milwaukee High School of the Arts) in 1921, as well as Ripon College from 1921-22.

FAMOUS AND NOT-SO-FAMOUS FILMS MADE IN WISCONSIN

Stroszek (Plainfield, 1977), a weird movie made by a weird German director Werner Herzog, based on Ed Gein's life. Ed Gein's 1957 ritual murders were the inspiration for *Psycho, The Texas Chainsaw Massacre, Silence of the Lambs*, and *Deranged*.

Damien: Omen II (Eagle river, 1978): Scary *Omen* sequel staring William Holden. There's a brutal ice-skating murder of old Lew Ayres.

F.I.S.T. (Mineral Point, 1978): Stallone's first after *Rocky*, written by Joe Ezsterhaus, one of the highest paid writers in the business at the time.

Mrs. Soffel (North Freedom, 1984).

Back to School (Madison, 1986): One of the few successful Rodney Dangerfield films, this was shot at the University of Wisconsin in Madison.

Major League (Milwaukee, 1989): Milwaukee County Stadium stood in for Cleveland Municipal Stadium; as many as 25,000 extras appeared in the scenes.

Gaily, Gaily (Milwaukee, 1968) was filmed in many pats of Milwaukee as part of the turn of the century background. A major scene was filmed at Forest Home Cemetery.

Family of Cops I, II, III (Milwaukee, 1996, 1998): written and produced by Joel Blasberg, which must have been fun for this former-Milwaukeean, has many street, river, and lakefront scenes recognizable to Milwaukeeans. It's about an improbable Jewish family of cops, headed by gruff Charles Bronson in a mellower mood (for Bronson).

WISCONSIN'S GIFTS TO HOLLYWOOD

The following actors, directors, and writers are from Wisconsin: Don Ameche (Kenosha), Eddie Cline (Kenosha) who worked with Buster Keaton and W.C. Fields as a writer and director; Ellen Corby (Racine), "Grandma Walton" from "The Waltons"; Ben Hecht (Racine), screenwriter; Carole Landis (Fairchild), Joseph Losey (La Crosse), Fred MacMurray (Beaver Dam), Fredric March (Racine), Pat O'Brien (Milwaukee), Gena Rowlands (Cambria), Orson Welles (Kenosha), Robert Bloch (Milwaukee), and many others.

From Jack Barth's *Roadside Hollywood*, 1991.

WHAT'S THERE TO SEE TODAY

Greta Garbo owned an apartment building in Milwaukee; Frank Lloyd Wright built a small apartment building and a Greek Orthodox Church in Milwaukee; Orson Welles's home in Kenosha is still standing on Seventh Avenue just off 61st Street plus there are many "Ameches" (Don Ameche) in the telephone book; Spencer Tracy's homes in Milwaukee include 2970 South Kinnickinnic Avenue and 2447 South Graham Street; Ben Hecht's homes in Racine include 1635 College, Bickel Street, and 827, later 823 Lake avenue; Ed Gein's farm house in Plainfield, just south of town, was burned down by locals; and Gene Wilder's, Charlotte Rae's and the Zucker/Abraham's homes are still standing in Milwaukee. Washington High School, on Sherman Boulevard, remains as it was. Wilder, class of '53, Tom Laughlin '49 and Joey Blasberg '63 were all graduates of the school as was Bud Selig, commissioner of baseball and Herb Kohl, U.S. Senator from Wisconsin, both Class of 1952. And me, Jackie Porter, class of '62, WHS, whose home at 2912 North 50th Street, at Locust, also still stands.

Directors/Writers: David Zucker, Jerry Zucker & Jim Abraham

BIBLIOGRAPHY

Barth, Jack, *Roadside Hollywood: The Movie Lover's State-by-State Guide to Film Locations, Celebrity Hangouts, Celluloid Tourist Attractions*, and *More*, Chicago, Ill: Contemporary Books, 1991. Paperback. Excellent guide.

Gabler, Neal, *An Empire of their Own: How the Jews Invented Hollywood*, New York: Crown Publishers, 1988. The classic book on the subject of Jews and Hollywood.

Gabler, Neal, Frank Rich, and Joyce Antler, *Television's Changing Image of American Jews*, New York: The American Jewish Committee and The Norman Lear Center, 2000. An analysis of the image of the Jew on TV as opposed to movies. Good comparative approach with important TV producers and writers interviewed.

Gurda, John, *One People, Many Paths: A History of Jewish Milwaukee*, Milwaukee, Wisc: Jewish Museum of Milwaukee, 2009. A fine history.

Hintz, Martin, *Images of America: Jewish Milwaukee*, Charleston, S.C.: Arcadia Publishing, 2005. A quickie book of photos slap-dashed together. Confusing though amusing.

Mitz, Rick, *The Great TV Sitcom Book*, New York: Richard Marek Publishers, 1980. See esp. pp. 321-326 (Happy Days) and various mentions of Charlotte Rae, pp. 177, 377, 418.

Moore, Deborah Dash, *To the Golden Cities: Pursuing the American dream in Miami and L.A.*, Cambridge, Mass.: Harvard University Press, 1994. Excellent book.

Movie Lot to Beachhead, compiled by the editors of *Look Magazine*, Garden City, New York: Doubleday, Doran and Company, 1945.

Porter, Jack Nusan with Gerry Glazer and Sandy Aronin, *Happy Days Revisited: Growing Up Jewish in Ike's America*, Newton, Mass.; The Spencer Press, 2010.

Stewart, Joseph, *TV and Video Almanac*, Santa Monica, CA: Santa Monica Press, 1997. See esp. pp. 126-128 on the "Happy Days" TV series (1974-1984).

Traxler, Ruth, '*The Golden Land': 150 Years of Jewish Life in Milwaukee*, Milwaukee, Wisc.: Sesquicentennial Celebration, 1994. See pp. 52-54 for Milwaukee's movie ties and pp. 13 and 60 for material on Jack Porter and his parents.

Visser, Kristin, revised by Diana Cook, *Wisconsin Trivia*, Nashville, Tenn.: Rutledge Hill Press (a Thomas Nelson Company), 1994, 2001.

Widen, Larry and Judi Anderson, *Silver Screens: A Pictorial History of Milwaukee's Movie Theaters*, Madison, WI: Wisconsin Historical Society Press, 2007.

Wilder, Gene, *Kiss Me Like a Stranger: My Search for Love and Art*, New York: St. Martin's Press, 2005.

DOCUMENTARIES

Imaginary Witness: Hollywood and the Holocaust directed by Daniel Anker; narrated by Gene Hackman, 2008. A movie that shows how Hollywood ignored he Holocaust during the war years and trivialized it afterwards. See Ty Burr's review of this film in the *Boston Globe*, Wednesday, January 2, 2008

Sources: Pacific Film Archives in Berkeley, Calif.; The Wisconsin State Historical Society; the Milwaukee Historical Society, the Milwaukee Jewish Historical Society; and the Wisconsin Center for Film and Media.

Answers to back cover trivia questions:

1. Washington High School, the same one that the author attended.

2. Who really knows? —somewhere in Milwaukee.

3. Maza

4. Nicolet High School, even though she lived on West Center Street;

5. Michael Jackson's estate—see, I told you'd never guess that.

PART TWO

SMALL TOWN SECRETS

PREFACE

I have tried here to address the secrets of Shoah
survivors and others in a small community of 22,000
Jews in Milwaukee. Actually this book has two parts:
the Shoah part and its secrets; and the general Jewish community and its tragedies. One part is about
the children of the Shoah and their parents, while
the other part is about the sudden death of rabbis
and young people, and the murder of ordinary Jews.
These are secrets that few knew about or scandals
that were kept quiet for decades, yet they affected me
growing up in Milwaukee.   Like an onion, you peel
away one layer and get more details, and then you
peel away more and more layers, and it gets more and
more fascinating and terrifyingly bizarre.

Death at an early age; not knowing who your father
was; suicides; tragic accidents. I still don't know all the
details. If you do know something I don't, like in the
famous TV show "Cops"—please tell me. Tell me the
truth, so I can revise and tell people before they die.
Otherwise the secret dies with us all.

The more I wrote about these events, the stranger
and more fascinating they became. For example, I

found one child of survivors who became a call girl in Los Angeles and another was a drug dealer for the Grateful Dead. But rather than titillation, I found a real need to uncover the "why" of these people, most of whom were childhood friends. Were these coping methods in dealing with a childhood that none had been prepared for—a post-Holocaust childhood? Why did we bond together in our small community? Who would understand us? The occasional outsider, even a fellow Jew, was often confounded. How could they understand when we ourselves didn't?

We tried to protect our parents. We idolized them; we also feared them. They had suffered so much. Strange. We loved them and feared them; feared they would take their love away from us; feared their anger, hurt, and shame and their dependence on us. We loved them and feared them and were angry at them, but could not show it, since they had "suffered" so much. Who was the "child," and who was the "parent"? It was a complex, confusing swirl of emotions. I am still in therapy decades later trying to understand it.

Why do I write about these secrets? Do I want to hurt anyone? No. The people involved are either dead or aging—in their 50's and 60's—what happened occurred a long time ago. The parents, for the most part, are dead or quite old. The hurt is still there and will never go away, but the story must be told. Maybe it can even help heal someone out there. Most are relieved that someone finally talked to them about it. A few wish not to discuss it with anyone. I respect their decision but then their story will be incomplete, such as in the case of Ayala or Fay. I couldn't get the entire picture of their lives and deaths, but I am sure in time I will.

I have changed the names of most of them except for Willi Rosman, Ayala Karsh, and Fay Robinson, since they have died and their stories are common knowledge in the survivor community. The others are still very much alive and good friends of mine so I had to protect their identities, and usually left things out. But I have done my best to conceal their identities. In some cases, they have allowed me to use their names if I concealed certain facts or if I state some facts but do not attribute it to them. I did send copies of what I wrote to several of the people mentioned here to get their reaction and to let them know what I was writing about. As I've said, for the most part, the response has been positive.

I wish to thank Howard Karsh, Serge Blasberg, Shelly Bankier, Arnie Peltz, Gloria (Golden) Sztundel, Ksiel Stzundel, Sandy Goldstein (Saundra Feher), Alice Robinson Lev, Milton Pivar, Andy Muchin, Gerry Glazer, Sandy Wendorf, Adam Pertman, and many others for their insights into these perplexing issues and past tragedies. Where there is an asterisk, the person's name is a pseudonym*, in order to protect his or her identity.

Write to me and tell me more or correct me when I went wrong: jacknusan@earthlink.net. Or call me anytime, night or day, (617) 965-8388 or my cell (857) 636-2669.

Dr. Jack Nusan Porter
Newtonville, Mass.
May 10, 2011

INTRODUCTION

The Holocaust of World War II still continues to impact us decades and generations later. Thirty years ago in 1981, I wrote in the *Journal of Psychology and Judaism* about a social and psychological "syndrome" that developed not only among the first generation of survivors, but also among the second generation. But I was overly optimistic about the second or even third generation. I later discovered even more angst and problems than I had foreseen, even extending to people into their 50's and 60's of the children of survivors, and perhaps into the third generation, though much milder. I was, to say the least, shocked at my findings.

I am speaking about the fifteen or so children of survivors (the so-called Next Gen or Second Gen) that I grew up with in Milwaukee, Wisconsin from the late 1940s to the late 1960s. I would be loath to extrapolate or generalize from this small sample to all Second Gen. Hopefully, researchers will follow-up my findings with a broader sample of US and Canadian children, with comparative samples in Israel, Europe, as well as perhaps South America, South Africa, Australia and New Zealand.

But in terms of Diaspora Second Gen, I see little differences; there may be some with Israeli Second Gen. It would be interesting to see how the Israeli experience, especially the army experience for "sabras," led to a difference. Also, what the difference between secular and *frum* (religious) Jews and less traditional Jews was; the difference between age cohorts and birth order also seems to me relevant here. The oldest male child seems to have suffered the most; and with each child later, the impact seems to be less severe. This has been one of my most important findings— birth order. The oldest male child usually had it the worst.

But I must emphasize that it has not stopped most of them from having useful, productive lives despite their afflictions. Still, the Shoah has affected some of their lives (and we are dealing here with people born from 1944-1955, from age 54-66 years of age in 2010).

THE CASE OF AYALA KARSH & FAY ROBINSON

I start with two of the most fascinating stories among this cohort of survivor's children: open secrets in the survivor community—concealed adoption.

My mother told me that two different daughters at different times came to her with the same story and said: "My mother won't tell me the truth; but she said: go to Mrs. Porter and she'll tell you!"

AYALA'S STORY

Let's take Ayala first. She was a beautiful, tall— six-foot—unusual for a Jewish woman to be so tall— olive-skinned, exotic, with statuesque breasts, and yet, she somehow knew that something was wrong. Her parents, Jacob and Janet Karsh, good friends to my parents, Irving and Faye Porter, were short, brown European Jews, looking nothing like their tall exotic daughter.

Sandy Aronin, in our book of memoirs *Happy Days Revisited*, has a gentle memory of Ayala:

"On my many visits home from *yeshiva*, I met Rabbi Michel Twerski's children's baby-sitter, Ayala. Ayala was a tall young lady, olive-skinned with a brilliant smile and a cute pointy nose. An Israeli, she had a cute accent, too." (2010: 92)

Ayala Karsh as a child (standing in front) with her father Jacob holding her. Janet Karsh to his left with her younger brother Aaron in the buggy. In Tel Aviv, near the beach and the Gat Rimon Hotel in the 1950's

Ayala's story went like this:

Ayala's father, a man named Kuznetsov, later re-named Kaufman, had been Janet's lover after the war and gotten her pregnant. They were both in displaced person's camps in Austria. He was a bit of scoundrel, an "unterveltkik" as they say in Yiddish. He told her to go to Palestine and that he would join her.

But he didn't. He left with another woman and went to Canada with a new wife and a new life. Janet was deeply insulted and hurt. Alone, pregnant, and angry, she met Jacob Karsh, a good decent man, in Tel Aviv in the late 1940s, and he agreed to "adopt" Ayala and keep the secret. That's the way it was back then—a big stigma.

Ayala was tortured her entire life that something was not "kosher"; why was her mother so angry at her? Who did she remind her of? And why didn't she look like Jacob?

Ayala in Los Angeles circa 2002

One day, she went to Mrs. Cyla Sztundel, a close family friend, and asked her: who am I? Who are my real parents? Mrs. Sztundel said: "You're not illegitimate. If you want to know, call Faygeh Porter," and she did, and my mother told her the truth.

Later, many years later, when Ayala was in her 50s, she killed herself, taking an overdose of drugs. But before that she was bi-polar—shifting from moody depression to angry outbursts. Before she died in about 2005, at age 60, she had alienated all of her closest friends.

According to Sandy Goldstein, one of those close friends, her entire personality changed. It was simply impossible to be with her anymore. She accused Sandy of all kinds of lies.

She stalked Al Rosen, a childhood friend, and a nice Jewish guy, a friend of mine, in LA; she destroyed that relationship. She called his mother and claimed that she was receiving Social Security payments "illegally," and that Al was "stealing" her money. All lies.

She got into debt; some say she owed money to the mob;

She got hooked on narcotics. She took anti-depressant drugs. Her son was a schizophrenic and lived with her in LA.

 A tragic ending.

Was her concealed adoption and identity a factor in her suicide? One will never know.

FAY'S STORY

I was lucky. I had the opportunity to interview Fay before she died of cancer in 2006 at age 65. Unlike Ayala, she died a natural death and she talked about her life. She was part of the Milwaukee survivor community, a bridge between the first and second generation; especially at the annual picnics in Kletzch Park, where they would come every summer. She gathered around her young and old and told them her story.

Fay's tale is similar yet very different from Ayala's. In both cases, daughter had violent fights and anger directed at mother for the lie. In Fay's case, her mother ran away when the war started to escape the Nazis while her lover Chaim was off at war in the Soviet army. So, Fay's father did not run away, but died in battle. Ayala's father ran off with another woman to Canada after he sent Ayala's mother to Palestine. However, in both cases, a young mother was faced with raising a child alone in those difficult post-war times when a woman without a man was unheard of.

When the Nazis were approaching the Soviet border, in Operation Barbarossa, Fay was born on July 22, 1941 in Novaya, near Odessa, Ukraine. Thus, she was conceived about November 1940. Operation Barbarossa, the invasion of Russia by the Nazis occurred on June 22, 1941, thus her father was killed in the very early part of that operation.

Fay's father was Chaim Koenig (later names include Koenigers and Gingiss). He knew of her coming birth and had even instructed Sarah to name the baby Funia after his dead sister. He left Sarah pregnant and died in battle, probably around late June or early July 1941, at the war's most furious, no doubt, before Fay (Funia) was born.

Chaim was a dapper, 24-year old with blue eyes, lovely lips, a strong nose, a very good looking man. And Fay also had the blond hair and blue eyes of her father; she was a true beauty, one of the most beautiful women I have ever met, and one of the nicest I have ever known, but while cordial to me and my mother, she was also very strong-willed. See photo with my mother.

Fay Robinson (on right) with my mother Faye Porter (1980's)

A SHORT BIOGRAPHY OF
MISHA (EPHRAIM MAYER) ROBINSON (RUBINZON)
BASED ON MATERIAL SUPPLIED TO ME
BY HIS DAUGHTER ALICE ROBINSON IN 1999

He was born on January 15, 1915, in Warsaw, Poland and died July 16, 1985, in Milwaukee and buried in Second Home Cemetery in Milwaukee. His occupation is listed as an agronomist, photographer, livestock dealer, and realtor. I knew him more as a livestock dealer but that work may have fizzled out. He was well educated for a survivor, having gone to the University of Nancy, in France from 1934 to 1938.

He married Mrs. Sarah Robinson on March 3, 1944 in Krivoy Rog, Ukraine, USSR, while the war was still raging. Her original name was Sarah Shpigel. They had three children: Fay (Fania), listed as "adopted" in a January 18, 1999 document, written by her sister Alice; Alice (Henia Efroimova), born in Romania on February 2, 1945; and Joe (Joseph Israel), born in Germany in August, 1946.

Mr. Robinson left Warsaw to study in France in 1934. He earned a degree in agronomy from the University of Nancy in 1938. He was becoming a French citizen and working for a dairy when his father suddenly died. He returned to Warsaw to liquidate the family business and move his brother and mother to France. However, six weeks after his arrival, on September 1, 1939, Hitler attacked Warsaw and World War II began.

Poland was defeated in two weeks, and he and his family were caught up in the war. When starvation and disease set in, he and a cousin escaped into Russia. His mother got papers to enter Russia but "disappeared" soon afterwards. His brother Lolek died while with the partisans, but the circumstances were not explained in the document .

Misha spent five years in the Soviet Union, during which time he met and married Sarah Shpigel Gingiss, a young, recently-widowed refugee from Bessarabia. He adopted Fay (Fania). They lived in Uzbekistan on a "sovchoz," a Russian collective farm. He worked breeding sheep and producing milk and cheese.

After the war, all refugees were directed to return to their places of origin. In December 1944, they returned to Sarah's grandfather's home in Romanovka, Bessarabia, and now Romania. Alice was born in that home. When she was six months old, the family traveled to Czechoslovakia. At the border, Jewish agents of the "Breichah" were waiting to help the refugees. They were sent to the Zeilsheim Displaced Person (DP) Camp in the American Zone. Zeilsheim was a housing project built by the Nazis for industrial workers of the chemical plant in Wiesbaden near Frankfurt am Main, Germany. It became a haven for Jewish refugees in 1945 under the United Nations UNRRA program. (Interestingly, my family and I were in a similar camp, also in housing built by the Nazis, but in Bindermichel, near Linz, Austria, not very far away, from about April 1945 to July 1946, when we received exit visas to come to America. I don't believe our families knew each other in Europe but met later in Milwaukee.)

Misha Robinson worked as a photographer (Foto Robinson) and the family lived comfortably. The last child, a son Joseph (Joey) was born there in August 1946. Misha made plans to immigrate to Palestine and use his agronomist skills there. However; the British had closed the borders to Jewish immigrants and they were stuck in Zeilsheim from 1945 to 1948.

There were plans to smuggle them out individually but Sarah did not want to separate the family again. Via a US soldier, the Robinsons got a message to an aunt and uncle in New York, papers were drawn up, and they arrived in the USA on October 30, 1948 on the S.S. General William Black. Fay was seven years old; Alice, three and a half; and Joe, two. Their names on the passenger list appeared as: Moniek, Sara, Fania, Henia, and Israel Rubinzon.

(My family had similar ambitions—to go to Palestine but due to my young age and the danger of a long arduous voyage, we decided to go to America instead and as luck would have it, we made contact with an uncle in Chicago also via a US soldier, and got out quite early, in July, 1946. Our ship was the S. S. Marine Perch. Others languished for years in the DP camps.)

The Robinsons lived with their uncle and aunt in Brooklyn for about six weeks. Misha decided that with his background in dairy agriculture, he was better off in Wisconsin, the "Dairy State", so they took a train to Wisconsin and settled in Milwaukee.

At first, they lived in an apartment downtown above Sherkow's Formalwear store at Third and State; then moved to a flat at 2141B North 10th Street for two and half years; to 14th Street, then 56th Street; and finally they bought a lot in suburban Glendale and built a home at 6601 North Bethmaur Lane. My family lived at 2125A North 10th Street, just south of North Avenue, and that is where our families met. (The "A" in an address refers to the rear entrance and the "B" to either another rear entrance or a detached house at the rear of the lot.)

FAY'S PERSPECTIVE

As noted, I had a poignant interview before Fay died of cancer in 2006 at age 65. As beautiful as ever, she would sit at the annual picnics in Klezch Park and counsel other young women up until she died. She was the wife of Dr. Alan Shlimovitz, a dentist. Here is her version of the story in her own words:

"Everyone in Milwaukee knew except me. I'll never feel better about my mother but we have to work it out. Why should I have good feelings about her? I experienced hurt in my family. One needs to respect my feelings!"

"Everything became a lie. When my mom lied to me about this, then everything else she told me was also a lie. My mother did not know the difference between truth and fantasy. She was a dominating person. She dominated and controlled everyone. I had to do everything the way she thought, and if I didn't do what she wanted, she would shout at me, "You don't appreciate what we did for you...even though your father is not your real father...."

"It was like I owed them everything. I was not a product of their marriage. I could have been left and put up for adoption. My mother would throw in my face that there were many people who left behind babies. She would tell me, "I saved your life" but in actuality, really I saved <u>her</u> life—being pregnant helped her to survive. She had to run and hide, to inculcate an instinct to live and to save my life as well.

She had to find a way to explain the loss of her husband and all this led to " dissonance," making up lies like if he died (her biological father Gingiss), when did he die? Where did he die? What's his yahrtzeit? Thus, more lies....

My mother was left with a lie and had to create further lies. Misha and Sarah had to make up a date of marriage and the 25th anniversary of their marriage. But the 25th was actually the 22 and half years....it created fantasies and more confusion.

Alice, my sister, was at my mom's death bed, and my mother showed her pictures of my father.

"I want you to bury them with me", she said to Alice.

But my sister didn't bury them; she gave them to me. It was then that I saw my "face" in his picture. I was blond but Misha (her non-biological father) was a "Spaniard", very dark, and my mom was Bessarabian...so where did the blondness come from?

I understood who I looked like—I had finally found my SELF!

I saw him in my children, in my second child, in his eyebrows....

I was left with a lie and so Misha and my mother had to create further lies...but lies eventually break down.

The other person in all this was of course Misha. Maybe it was Misha—his male ego was threatened—if he told the truth, he thought he'd be the "outsider" because of that bond between me and my mom. So, Misha suggested this "lie" to my mom.

There was never any equality among European refugees. The man was the Lord but the woman pulled the strings underneath.

Finally, I confronted my mother and she said—go ask Mrs. Porter and she'll tell you, and I did, and your mother told me sadly that it was true, that all the mothers and fathers in the community knew but were sworn to secrecy.

Chaim Gingiss, my father. It's ironic that I named one of my children after Misha's father, who was also named Chaim.

A cousin of our's told my sister Alice that she knew my natural father's brother, but it turned out not to be a brother but a cousin—Koeniger.

But from that discovery, I eventually tracked down my father's family.

Yet, Alice, her sister, disagrees and has written me, saying: "There are two sides to this story; not everything that Fay says is truthful..." I would like to hear more from Alice's side and tell her story as well. She did write to me again in 2007 and said: "...you should always consider the personal and private sensibilities of the individual lives you are delving into...Regarding my family, my only comment is that like all parents,...they did the best they could with what they knew at the time. I have no further information to contribute. Sincerely, Alice Lev."

Fay Robinson Shlimovitz also threw out another theory to me in my interview with her, of survivor's behavior caused by deprivation of food; that there were pancreas and insulin problems: stressed out pancreas that shot out too much insulin into the body which led to fluctuations of sugar metabolism. Too much of a high or too much of a low can be a problem. (The "greeneh," the Jewish refugees, had certain personality traits for the most part, especially the women they were quick-tempered, easily insulted, and then went into depression, melancholy or mood swings.) Fay was not diabetic but felt she improperly metabolized sugar. This condition is called hypoglycemia and can lead to diabetes.

When you look at "greeneh", she noted, many share those traits noted above. This aspect of survivors should be looked at. Many had anger problems—men and women—and we can't simply blame the "war" or the "camps"; no, that is insufficient. We have to look at medical issues, Fay said.

This was her theory, not mine. It continues to be controversial.

My interpretation: You can't blame Sarah and Misha entirely. Such were the times. Not telling children was the case in those days. Unwed mothers were a scandal and were stigmatized. A man was needed to protect a woman. A woman alone, pregnant or with a baby, was not simply pitied, as if she were to blame, but also in great danger from rape or harassment by Russian soldiers and others.

I know there were hurt and anger on the child's part, and shame and guilt on the mother's part. However, in Jewish law, there is the notion of "kuvid av va'em," honor thy father and mother; it does not say to "love them," only to "honor them," don't shame them. Sarah Robinson deserved more love and attention than she got in life. *Kuvid* is more important than love in this situation.

The same was true for Ayala and her mother Janet. All her life Ayala was made aware of the differences between her tall exotic, olive skin and black eyes and her short brown-haired parents. Times have changed and now, thankfully, people are told about their biological parents in most cases.

The media has very rarely dealt with the issue of birth secrets, adoption issues, etc. The best one ironically was a comedy by Woody Allen—*Mighty Aphrodite* starring Mina Sorvino, whose endearing performance won her an Academy Award for supporting actress. The movie actually shows the opposite: a father (Allen) who wants to know about his adopted son's real mother (Sorvino) amidst tension and martial problems with his wife (played by Helen Bonham-Carter).

Toward the tail end of writing this book, I met Adam Pertman, director of the Adoption Institute and he shared many insights with me about such "concealed" or "closed" adoptions.

Life is complicated. But secrets hurt and continue to hurt.

SUICIDE: WILLI ROSMAN AND AYALA KARSH

As I have written elsewhere, suicide is quite rare among Holocaust survivors and even rarer for their children. (See my essay "Holocaust Suicides" in my book *The Genocidal Mind*, 2006). Thus two suicides in a small community of survivors in the Jewish community of Milwaukee of only 20,000 Jews with less than a thousand Shoah survivors is a phenomenon that needs to be studied.

And yet, like so many of the subjects and issues in this book, we know very little about their suicides. Take Willi Rosman, a likeable yet intense young man. I know him mostly throughout my teens—he was dark-haired, somewhat pudgy, with a slightly mis-shapen nose—a nice fellow yet one who was always trying to fit in. I have a picture of him at my bar mitzvah. His folks were survivors like mine but with a difference. His father was quiet but his mother was intense, a typical or better yet, stereotypical Jewish mother—always pushing her kids (he had a younger brother named Albert), pushing food on us like Mrs. Cyla Sztundel, warmhearted but intense, much more so than my own mom.

And she was very protective. "Willi, wear your scarf; Willi, put on your boots; Willi, be careful out there. Again, very "normal" for Shoah survivors. They had few kids, and these were often "replacement children" for the dead. Each child was precious and had to be "protected".

There's a photo of Willi on page 13 of my earlier memoir, Happy Days Revisited. There's also a photo of him in the January 1961 Washington H.S. Yearbook on page 118.

And as per my theory, the oldest male got it the worst. Howard Karsh, a social worker who worked with Shoah children, said it best: "Willi had a classic, overbearing, guilt-inducing mother and a weak father." Again, I would say that Mr. Rosman was not "weak" but he did not or could not stop his wife's way of raising the children. Perhaps, 'distant" rather than "weak" is a better adjective. My father was far from "weak" but somewhat "distant"; mothers raised the children. The man worked and brought home the "corned beef" (not the pork); and the mother raised the children. The fathers were emotionally distant and the mothers were emotionally smothering.

HOWARD KARSH'S VIEW

Howard Karsh was a respected social worker and youth worker in Milwaukee, who worked with many children of survivors over the years. Later, he was (and is still) a leader on the West Side, Sherman Park area neighborhood. These are his words:

Shoah parents delayed their children's adolescence. They could not accept their growing up, marrying, and moving away. They wanted to "protect" them but could not.

They gave their children a mixed message: be free and independent; do what ever you want, but only marry a Jewish person and "stuck" Jewish.

Larry Weidenbaum, a Shoah parent, for example, spoiled his kids and allowed them to date <u>shiksehs</u> (non-Jewish women) but got mad when they married one.

The kids didn't know what to do because the parents didn't know how to raise American kids. They didn't know whether to be strict or not. Mothers were hysterical regarding their children and were too close to them.

The boys got it worse because the parents didn't know what they wanted from them. The girls got it easier and were ignored. All they had to do was get married and have kids. The parents had no big ambitions for them.

Problems were rife: Danny Goldberg* was bi-polar; Robert Nelson* became an addict; and people like Willi became severely mentally ill, let out of mental hospitals when they were not ready to be let out.

People had to leave town in order to survive, many going to the coasts—California, New York, or Boston. The first sons got it worst; the younger sons less so. The fathers were very hard on their first-born sons. They had high expectations on the first son, easier on the second or third or on their daughters.

Everyone was a victim. The women were often "stuck". Mrs. Sztundel for example felt indebted to her husband Avrum for protecting her after the war by marrying her and guilty for the loss of his wife and young son. She was so intense that she drove her children as far away as they could go on the continent—San Francisco. They could have only survived if they left.

"Your mom (speaking to me) saw herself as a soldier, and your dad spoke and acted like a warrior, not a victim".

Willi never was able to get away. He was in a mental hospital but they made a mistake in letting him out. He felt Nazis were after him and he stole spoons. He was under a lot of sedation and then killed himself to get rid of the pain.

AYALA'S SUICIDE

While Willi killed himself to get rid the pain and guilt that his mother laid on him, Ayala's death was more complex and had multiple causes. The problem is that neither her former husband David Wabyick nor any of her children could I even trace down, let alone talk to. I could only rely on her closest friends—Sandy Goldstein, Steve Cohen, and a few others. The last time I saw her can be seen in the photo I took in Malibu at a party. (See p. 59)

Was her "concealed birth" a factor in her death? Perhaps, it was an underlying contributing factor, but I think the real reason was more complex and a classic combination of reasons for suicide—unrequited love, a breakup, a poor self image, confusion over the future, few self-controls, little guidance, paranoia, isolation, business failures, and increased debt.

Again, like Willi, there were numerous signs to get her help. Willi stole spoons and acted bizarrely; Ayala got very angry and acted bizarrely, to the point where even her most faithful friends fled. Fore example, she fell in love with one of our childhood friends, Al Rosen, the former husband of Jerri Sussman, sister to my childhood friend Lyle Sussman.

However, it became overbearing. She stalked him at work; phoned him obsessively, and when he objected, she started spreading rumors that he was "embezzling" money. She did the same with her closest friend Sandy Goldstein Feher. She threatened to "expose" certain business secrets she knew about Sandy, and Sandy had to cut off the relationship.

She incurred bad debts and some creditors came after her personally and she might have been threatened. She lived beyond her means.

Ironically, the pictures show her in a happy mood. She did seem very gaunt and thin; the young beauty described by Sandy Aronin in my first memoir *Happy Days Revisited* had changed but still she was upbeat and energetic.

We had a great party at her beach house in Malibu. It was the same condo complex where Charlie Sheen lived. I even met a beautiful woman, the former wife of a Hollywood director, who directed the movie *The Revolutionary* and we had a bit of tryst; I wish I could remember her name.

It was the last time I saw her alive. She left behind several children, some living in Milwaukee, one in California, a sister Rivkeh Karsh living in Chicago and her former husband David Wabyick, living in Milwaukee. I was unable to contact any of her immediate family.

Sexual Abuse/Incest

The bête noir of our civilization. Totally unknown, totally taboo to talk about it. We simply don't know enough about these sensitive topics but they are emerging. However, one interesting factoid. There are enough female Shoah children to have organized a group of Lesbian Children of the Holocaust. It is a real organization consisting of daughters of Holocaust survivors. Though not all lesbians have attributed sexual abuse or the Holocaust as a factor in their lesbianism, it could be a factor. Of course, the stories of sexual abuse by rabbis have been documented but these have most often been against boys in their late teens or against adult women. Still, no study that I know of has been done of daughters of Shoah survivors and their abuse and later gender identity. I would love to hear from readers with both anecdotal material and scientific studies.

Still, sexual abuse definitely exists in the Jewish community; it's just hidden better.

Prostitution

As for prostitution, I came across one case of a child of survivors who allegedly engaged in prostitution. She was a call girl in LA. LA seemed a good place for people from Milwaukee to disappear to and start a new life, far from prying eyes. Elena,*(see p. 53) as I will call her, was a thin, beautiful, striking girl with a twin sister. I have kept her name and identity out of this book. I also have very little background on why and how. The only thing I know was that she is dead and that I grew up with her and knew her. There were

72

dysfunctional elements in her life but I do not have any answers. Her twin sister is still alive and could comment more if she wishes to. I know how to reach her.

THE MURDER OF MRS. SYLVIA FINK ON SEPTEMBER 19, 1959

The murder of Mrs. Sylvia Fink was so profound in my life and in Milwaukee's life that I stop my diary in September 1959 because of it and Norman Schumacher's death. It was all over the front pages of the *Milwaukee Journal* and *Milwaukee Sentinel* (these were the days before they had merged into one paper—the *Journal-Sentinel*).

Again, it was sudden and bizarre and the work of a mentally ill person, illegally released from a hospital. Could it be in those days, they did not have the psychotropic medicine they have today that could have curbed the bizarre thoughts and violent acts that so disturbed these sad, deranged people? Plus it was a black man, a "Negro" as they called them back then, who did the killing.

The Parness killings seven years earlier in the inner city (the "black ghetto") and the Sylvia Fink killing were similar in that both perpetrators were deranged black men who should have been either institutionalized or deeply medicated. In the Parness case, it has-

tened the exodus of the inner city Jews to the suburbs
and to the West Side; and the Fink killing did that as
well, but from the West Side to the outer suburbs.
These crimes unsettled the Jewish community. Life
would never be the same again; a mere four years
later, President John F. Kennedy would be murdered
in Dallas, and our world, no, our civilization, would
never be the same again.

Here is the story:

On the front page of *The Milwaukee Journal*, on
Tuesday, September 22, 1959, was splashed across six
columns, the words: "School Aide's Wife Found Slain;
Seek Suspect Seen Near Home" and inside: "Killer
Shoots His Way into Fink House" and "Life Was Just
Getting Brighter; Then Tragedy Comes to Finks."

Life was getting better. Jews and other middle class
whites had escaped from the inner city in the 40's and
50's and were filling up the sun-splashed northwest
side of Milwaukee with its good schools, green parks,
and open space.

But the ghetto would not disappear. In both cases,
the killer was a young black male with serious psychological problems, who should have been incarcerated
in a mental hospital but wasn't. Also, hand guns and
rifles were readily available.

There was also a huge display of pictures. Here is
the lead paragraph:

"A Negro believed by police to be the slayer of
Mrs. Sylvia Fink. 39, wife of a city school official, was
sought Tuesday."

"The body of Mrs. Fink was found by her 11 year old daughter Michele, lying on the kitchen floor of the home at 3902 N. 64th Street, when the girl returned from school about 3:30 p.m. Monday."

"Mrs. Fink was the wife of Herbert W., 44; vice-principal of the Brown Street School, 2029 N. 20th St. The school has Negro pupils."

"Mrs. Fink had been shot twice."

The killer, Roscoe Simpson, 30, was an ex-mental patient, described as a religious "fanatic" and a lay preacher, by acquaintances. He was walking about the neighborhood talking "irrationally" about the Gospel and about being a minister. At each home, he asked to speak to "the lady of the house."

He was killed the very next evening. Rather than run away, he again walked around the neighborhood with a five gallon gasoline can, half full of gasoline, a box of matches, and a .38 caliber police special revolver believed to have been the same gun which killed Mrs. Fink. He had around his waist a cartridge belt which carried 25 extra cartridges and there were 11 loose cartridges in his trouser's pocket. He was the father of six children, and his wife Tomato, 28, was expecting her seventh.

Simpson apparently got upset with something that Mrs. Fink said to him, pulled out his gun and shot her through the locked front screen door, followed the already wounded woman to the kitchen, and then fired the death shot in her kitchen. It was around 1 PM in broad daylight.

The shootout on Tuesday was also quite a tragedy. Simpson was shot eight times, one bullet piercing his heart. However, Police Sgt. Raymond Nencki was

78

shot in the neck and abdomen by Simpson. Police said Simpson, when confronted, fired first and then fell, fatally   wounded by bullets fired by Patrolman Joseph Friday, the second time as Simpson lay dying on the ground.

Tuesday night's gun battle occurred in an alley alongside 3954 N. 63rd Street, just one block from the Fink home. Abraham Hansher, 63, and his wife, Mary, 48, were witnesses and saw the gunman with his gun and the police closing in on him.

The policemen survived the gunfight. Mr. Fink's school was shocked and saddened. The Brown Street School was proud of its racial harmony. Susie Fink, my childhood friend, married and eventually moved away to Connecticut.

THE TRIPLE MURDER OF
BERNARD AND FANNIE PARNESS
AND THEIR EMPLOYEE IRWIN LUICK
ON NOVEMBER 8, 1952.

The Parness murders were likewise bizarre, and
again it was front page news, splashed across three
columns in the Saturday, November 8, 1952, issue of
the *Milwaukee Journal*, about seven years before the
Fink killing. However there were important differences. First, the killing took place in the inner city, not
the white outer areas of Milwaukee. Second, the killer
immediately laid down his two rifles and surrendered
to police. Thus, he could still be alive today. But the
similarities are also eerie. Both men were black men in
their early 30s; both well-dressed; both mentally deranged. Bernard Parness, president of Sterling Clean-
ers, and his wife, Fannie, secretary of the firm, and
both about 52 years old, owned a dry cleaning store in
the inner city.

The killings took place about 12:30 p.m. on a Saturday at the dry cleaning shop at 1800 N. 4th St. The
Parnesses lived at 3179 N. 50th Street. (Two blocks
from my house at 2912 N. 50th Street). The crimes
were admitted by Clorise L. Walls, 32, of 2425 N. 11th

St. Walls killed the Parnesses and another man, an employee, because he was upset about the cleaning of his pants!

As the account said: "When brought to the Safety Building, Walls told police and reporters: "I shot those people for personal reasons, over an argument about cleaning clothes".

He was arrested by Patrolman Walters at about N. 3rd St. and W. Reservoir, when he saw Walls approaching him with two rifles under his arm.

Walters shouted: "Lay down those rifles!" Walls complied. Walls told the officer: "I just shot three persons. I don't want any more trouble…I shot for personal reasons. Really, I'm just a murderer. I'm a murderer. I shot three people".

All three were pronounced dead on arrival at the County Emergency Hospital. The two rifles carried by Walls were a .30-.30 and a .22 caliber. In his possession, police also found about 200 cartridges for a .22 rifle and three boxes of ammunition for the .30-.30 rifle.

Walls had just come from Bessemer, Alabama about September 1. He had bought the .30-.30 in Ogden, Utah for $104.40.

It was the biggest slaying case in Milwaukee since Joseph Arnold Schulz, 16, killed his mother, sister, and brother the winter before.

And all it was about an argument over a pair of pants.

Their son, Eugene Parness, a Habonim youth leader, left Milwaukee and moved to a kibbutz in Israel, where he lives to this day.

The Sylvia Fink murder was big headline news, exacerbated by the hunt for the killer and the police shooting him down within hours of the murder in the back alley of a staid middle-class area where we all lived. I am sure that it hastened the exodus of Jews out of the Northwest side of Milwaukee to the safer suburbs of Shorewood, Whitefish Bay, Fox Point, Glendale, and Mequon. It increased the debate over both gun control and the treatment (or better yet, the "non-treatment") of the mentally ill. Today, perhaps, with better drugs, many of these crimes could have been avoided.

The murders also exacerbated black-white and black-Jewish tensions, and led to white flight. But the biggest trauma was to all involved: the Fink and Parness families, their children, and friends; the perpetrators' families and their children; the policemen shot; and the entire community of the West Side. Today, Milwaukee is, like many American cities, almost entirely segregated into a white suburbia and a majority black inner city. And the violence continues.

Rabbi Dudley Weinberg

THE SUICIDES OF
RABBI DUDLEY WEINBERG &
RABBI AVIE WAXMAN

RABBI DUDLEY WEINBERG

Rabbi Dudley Weinberg's suicide at age 60 on May 19, 1976 shocked the entire Milwaukee community and made front-page news. The rabbi was extremely well-known for his forceful sermons especially in the wake of the civil rights movement. He was a powerful speaker and a nationally known theologian and rabbinic leader. And it was prominently written that it was indeed a suicide when so often, such acts are papered over and denied. Interesting to contrast, just ten years later, the suicide of another rabbi, Avie Waxman, age 46, who died August 19th, 1985, was not mentioned as a suicide. And the same with Willi Rosman, age 54, who died August 3rd, 1997 and Ayala Karsh who died about a decade later; they were not publicly reported suicides. In any case, Rabbi Weinberg's sudden death was the most well-known of them all, given his stature in the Jewish community, the city, and the nation.

The *Milwaukee Journal* headline shouted: "Rabbi Weinberg Found Dead Just Before Return to Pulpit";

Rabbi Weinberg Found Dead Just Before Return to Pulpit

Rabbi Dudley Weinberg of Congregation Emanu-El B'ne Jeshurn was dead on arrival at Columbia Hospital Wednesday afternoon after being found in a car in his garage.

The rabbi, 60, was to have returned to the pulpit Friday night after being absent since June.

According to the medical examiner's report, Weinberg had been under psychiatric care for depression and was being treated for a severe cardiac condition.

His wife found him in her car in their garage at 1100 E. Lexington Blvd., Whitefish Bay, shortly after 5 p.m. He was dead on arrival at 5:23 p.m.

According to the medical examiner, the motor of the auto was not running, although the ignition was on, and the gasoline tank was full. The garage door was reportedly closed but not locked, and the driver's side window was down.

The report said Weinberg had made reservations to take his wife to dinner Wednesday night. Mrs. Weinberg had been at work since early morning.

She said Wednesday night that his Friday sermon was prepared and typed.

An autopsy was to be performed Thursday.

As rabbi of the oldest Reform congregation in the Milwaukee area, Weinberg was outspoken in his espousal of liberal causes, such as racial justice, opposition to the Indochina war and rights for Soviet Jewry.

He set the tone in his inaugural sermon on Sept. 9, 1955, at Congregation Emanu-el.

In a year of French Presidentiousing marches.

RABBI WEINBERG

—Sentinel Photo

heyday, when many intellectuals were suspected of being "Communist dupes," Weinberg told his congregation:

"If I ever hear of your talking about an 'egghead' or in any way disparaging our teachers, you will get my dander up."

Booming Voice

This he declared in a deep, booming voice that made him one of the most forceful pulpiteers in the city. His sermons and even conversation were serious in tone, with little informality or levity.

During the 1960s he was a founder and later president of the Greater Milwaukee Conference on Religion and Race.

In September, 1963, at the Religion and Race Rally, he and five other clergymen of different faiths took a pledge to work for the elimination of racism.

As the racial equality campaign gained steam in the 1960s he supported Father James E. Groppi in his open housing marches.

He once called for "radicalism" instead of "liberalism" as a civil rights stance, and scolded the religion and race organization for "ducking the issues." Nevertheless, the group elected him chairman in 1968.

Besides taking an interest in the city's art and culture, Weinberg also helped educate Milwaukee clergy and others about Judaism.

Used Institute

This was done through the annual Institute on Judaism at Temple Emanu-el and through frequent talks to ministerial groups.

He was the first rabbi to permit a reporter to cover a High Holiday service.

He also sought to educate his own congregation on other religions.

In 1964 he invited Archbishop William E. Cousins to talk at Temple Emanu-el on Vatican II. This is believed to be the first time a Milwaukee archbishop had spoken in a Jewish congregation.

He maintained friendship with Cousins and other church leaders, but in 1965, when Roman Catholics protested the request of $50,000 in antipoverty funds to establish Planned Parenthood clinics, Weinberg cautioned against letting the birth control controversy get out of hand by becoming "an angry argument."

Stressed Individual

Weinberg recommended, "We can insist on the freedom of each individual to act in accordance with that moral and religious authority which he conscientiously recognizes.

He was also president and

Turn to Page 16, Col. 2

Rabbi Found Dead

Continued From Page 5

founder of the Wisconsin Council of Rabbis, member of the Governor's Committee on the United Nations, the planning committee of the Milwaukee United Community Services, the Milwaukee Anti-Poverty Board and the former Marquette University Medical School Committee on Medicine and Religion.

His support of Jewry abroad ranged from pleadings in behalf of the right of Jews in the Soviet Union to emigrate to Israel to frequent visits to Israel.

In 1969, as chairman of the United Jewish Appeal Rabbinical Advisory Committee, he headed a fact finding visit of more than 100 American rabbis to Israel.

Opposed War

The Vietnam War was another of his international interests.

One of his last appearances took place in January, 1973, at St. Matthew Catholic Church at an antiwar rally.

He drew applause from the 400 participants as he declared that "the blood of the bombings must be washed from our hands," and called for an immediate halt to "this unspeakable destruction."

His rabbinical associations included service on the executive board of the Central Conference of American Rabbis (CCAR), as a trustee of the Union of America: Hebrew Congregation (UAHC) and chairman of the CCAR-UAHC Joint Commission on Worship.

On Liturgy Panel

He was also a member of the 14 member CCAR Liturgy Committee, which produced the New Union Haggadah for Passover services, a guide which was released early in March.

Weinberg came to Temple Emanu-el from Temple Ohabei Shalom in Boston, Mass., which he served from 1946 to 1955.

Born in St. Louis, Mo., he earned degrees from Carleton College, Northfield, Minn., and Hebrew Union College, Cincinnati, Ohio, which in 1966 awarded him a doctor of divinity degree.

He saw World War II service as a major in the chaplains corps.

Besides his wife, Marian, he is survived by two sons, Avrom, Belmont, Mass., and Jonathan, New Haven, Conn.; a daughter, Miss Myra Weinberg, Cambridge, Mass., and a brother, Melvin, St. Louis, Mo.

Funeral arrangements were pending.

"Rabbi's Death May Be a Suicide"; "Rabbi Found Dead"; and from the Wisconsin Jewish chronicle, May 27, 1976: "Community Mourns Rabbi's Death"; "Weinberg Affected Many Lives" ; and "Old friends Gather for Weinberg Funeral" (*Milwaukee Sentinel*, Saturday, May 22, 1976).

On June 3, 1976, prominent editor and columnist, Edwarde F. Perlson in the *Wisconsin Jewish Chronicle*, wrote a moving, page-long column noting the 900-plus mourners who crowded the great hall of the city's largest Reform temple, Emanu-El B'nei Jeshurun.

The outpouring of grief was huge. Rabbi Weinberg was a dynamic and superbly gifted orator—a kind of Jewish Martin Luther King—as the articles show. His deep booming voice made him a forceful leader in the community. He was especially active in civil rights, courageously supporting Father James E. Groppi's open housing marches on the South Side. He was active in the anti-Vietnam movement, rare for a rabbi then, and in inter-religious affairs with Catholics and Protestants.

At his funeral, to his Reform Temple, probably for the first and last time, came Orthodox rabbis such as Rabbi Michel Twerski of Congregation Beth Jehudah and Rabbi Israel Feldman of Congregation Agudas Achim as well as other Milwaukee Conservative and Reform rabbis. Rabbi Arthur Lelyveld of Cleveland, Ohio, president of the Central Conference of American Rabbis spoke as well as Rabbi Lou Silberman and Rabbi F. Barry Silberg, Emanu-el's associate rabbi.

The cause of suicide is often unknown. Most likely, it was deep depression. Back then, as you can see, the papers were not afraid to state that it was indeed

88

THE WISCONSIN JEWISH CHRONICLE   May 27, 1976

Community Mourns Rabbi's Death

Rabbi Dudley Weinberg, 60, of Temple Emanu-El B'ne Jeshurun, died May 19, two days before he was to re-ascend the pulpit of the largest synagogue in the state.

For the past year, Weinberg had been on leave from the Temple.

Weinberg had been in poor health, having had a history of heart disease.

In statements by several leaders of the Milwaukee religious community, both Jewish and Christian, a sense of loss caused by Weinberg's untimely death was expressed.

Archbishop William E. Cousins, spiritual leader of the Catholic Church in Milwaukee, said that the community has lost a real leader, not only in his liberal thought but also in his association with the community.

"He had a concern and a comprehensive compassion for people in general," the Archbishop said. "He left his impact, and he will be rewarded for his dedication."

Rabbi Francis Barry Silberg, associate rabbi of Emanu-El, said the death is a loss "for our people of a beacon and a bellweather.

"Dudley Weinberg was not only a man in the purest sense, he was the Jewish soul crying out for truth, compassion and justice."

Many of the rabbi's activities were concerned with human rights, both at home and abroad. Active within the United Jewish Appeal — he was chairman of that group's Rabbinical Advisory Committee — he worked for the rights of Soviet Jews as well as equal housing in Milwaukee.

His interests spanned not only the range of activities within the Milwaukee Jewish community, but he also was concerned with relations between the faiths, a concern which brought about a friendship between himself and Cousins.

Within the Jewish community, he formed the Wisconsin Council of Rabbis, taught in and guided the religious school activities at Emanu-El as well as stabilizing that congregation's membership after two successive break-away groups formed other Reform temples.

"He spent a lot of time in study," said Rabbi Jay Brickman, of Temple Sinai. "He was a fine educator and a gifted teacher."

One of Weinberg's greatest concerns within the Jewish community here was for the establishment of a Reform day school, a dream which he never saw fulfilled.

Until his death he was working on commentary for the Book of Deuteronomy, having been selected for the work by a national committee.

(Continued on Page 15)

Weinberg Affected Many Lives

(Continued from Page 1)

Weinberg had served on the executive committee of the Central Conference of American Rabbis, the Reform organization in the United States. The CCAR had also chosen him to help write a new prayerbook, which had been completed some time ago.

Another of his progressive and innovative actions included allowing a newspaper reporter to cover High Holiday services.

"He has made an indelible impression," Rabbi Harry Pastor said, "and an ineradicable impact on the lives of his congregation and of many individuals beyond those confines."

"In the span of years granted to him he achieved many times more than others who might outlive him by decades," Pastor continued.

Besides his scholarship and his dedication to human rights, Weinberg was instrumental in averting a move of the Congregation to a Fox Point location.

At ground breaking ceremonies for an addition to the Temple almost two years ago, Weinberg said the addition was to provide "room for the spirit as well as room for the bodies. Emanu-El has always been an urban congregation with urban concerns." This statement reaffirmed his own intention to continue with activist stands.

The rabbi is survived by his wife, Marian, two sons, Avrom of Belmont, Mass., and Johnathan, of New Haven, Conn.; a daughter, Miss Myra Weinberg, of Cambridge, Mass., and a brother Melvin, of St. Louis, Mo.

He had a great dedication to people and concern for others. Rabbi Herbert Panitch, past president of the Wisconsin Council of Rabbis said that it would be "hard to see life without him."

"I will personally miss him more than I can say," said Silberg, "because I loved him very very much. He was my brother, truly my brother."

"He left his impact," said Cousins. "It is one not to be copied."

"We shall surely miss him," said Pastor. "We are eternally grateful for having had him."

Brickman, perhaps, summed it up best, saying "He was a Jew for all seasons."

Milwaukee Memories

Old Friends Gather for Weinberg Funeral

By JAMES M. JOHNSTON
Sentinel Religion Editor

Old friends in the Jewish clergy recalled the richness with which Rabbi Dudley Weinberg filled their lives in a 45 minute ceremony Friday at the temple whose congregation he had led for more than 20 years.

Weinberg, 60, was buried in Greenwood Cemetery after the funeral at Temple Emanuel B'ne Jeshurun, 2419 E. Kenwood Blvd., just 35 years after his ordination. He died Wednesday. About 900 persons sat in the main floor and balcony of the temple auditorium.

"He was taken from us when he was far too young," said Rabbi Arthur J. Lelyveld of Cleveland, Ohio, president of the Central Conference of American Rabbis.

Seminary Friends

Rabbi Lou J. Silberman of Nashville, Tenn., who had known him 40 years, declared that his old friend from their days at Hebrew Union Seminary "was brought all too soon to the moment beyond our claim."

Both rabbis recalled Weinberg's lighter side, which seldom came through from his pulpit or in his public talks in which he thundered against the injustices of the day.

"His gift for fun and mimicry, his zest for life enriched the companionship of our student days," said Lelyveld, who was also a schoolmate.

"He was a scholar, and when a scholar dies we are all hereft, for we are all his relatives," said Lelyveld. "This congregation is bereft, as is the American Jewish Community and the Central Conference of American Rabbis," Lelyveld added.

"Dudley Weinberg was a rabbi's rabbi," Lelyveld said.

Silberman said Weinberg's "mind was sensitive, though vigorous and his intellectual appetite insatiable."

"How often, during our school days, when we perplexed about studies, did he pick up his fiddle and fill our study with melody! How often this would banish care and send our spirits back to our studies!"

Others Present

Among the 900 was the Milwaukee Jewish clergy, those of the Orthodox and Conservative branches, some of whom seldom enter a Reform synagog like Emanu-el, wore the yarmulke, or small skull cap. Two rabbis, Michael Twersky of Congregation Beth Jehuda and Israel Feldman of Congregation Agudas Achim, wore their long black coats and black hats.

Sitting with them in a body were Rabbis Louis J. Swichkow of Beth El Ner Tamid, Bernard Reichman of Anshai Lebowitz, Herbert G. Panitch of Beth Israel and Isaac N. Lerer of Temple Menorah.

Nearby sat Reform Rabbis Harry B. Pastor of Shalom and Jay R. Brickman of Sinai.

Non-Jewish clergy also attended — the Rev. John W. Cyrus of the First Unitarian Church and several priests with Roman collars. Also present was James E. Groppi, whom Weinberg had supported in his open housing marches in 1967.

Emanu-el's associate rabbi, F. Barry Silberg who had led the congregation during the last several months during Weinberg's illness, conducted the rite in a mixture of Hebrew and English.

90

suicide. He was found dead in his garage with the car warm, as if it had been running. The ignition key was on and the garage door was reportedly closed. He had been under psychiatric care for depression and was being treated for a severe cardiac condition. His wife found him in the car on Wednesday. His sermon for Friday night was prepared, typed and ready to be delivered.

RABBI AVIE WAXMAN

Rabbi Avie Waxman's suicide at the age of 46 on August 19, 1985 about a decade after Rabbi Weinberg was less significant city-wide but was still deeply felt within the Milwaukee Jewish community. Rabbi Waxman and his first wife Rena Waxman were very popular and beloved figures in the Jewish and general communities, where he was a teacher and role model for many young people. They had two daughters Shifra and Hadassah and three sons Hillel, Mayer, and David; his mother was Sarah Waxman of Israel; he had a sister Shulamith (Abraham) Lebowitz of Israel; and a brother, the noted sociologist Dr. Chaim (Chaya) Waxman of New York and later also of Israel. Waxman was related to a very distinguished family of rabbis and scholars.

After his divorce from Rena, he married Linda Raymond, a musician.

Graveside services were held in Mount Zion Cemetery in Milwaukee with Rabbis Tsvi Schur and David Eisenbach officiating.

What is interesting in his obituary in the *Wisconsin Jewish Chronicle* of August 30, 1985, is that it describes him as "the only Milwaukee rabbi who would officiate at interfaith marriages" and also as an insurance agent and part-time rabbi at Congregation Emanu-El of Waukesha, a Reform synagogue founded in 1939.

An earlier article dated August 11, 1977 from the *Chronicle* had even more complex background. He was described as a college professor of psychology and Judaic Studies at Holy Redeemer College, a school psychologist at the Milwaukee Public Schools, principal of Hillel academy in 1969-1970; and then accepted a position as Director of the Jewish Community Day School in Palm Beach County, Florida. He later returned to Milwaukee.

THE SUDDEN DEATH OF NORMAN SCHUMACHER

While there have been other tragic deaths in this community—Baki Muchin the most recent, none affected me as much as Norman Schumacher's death at age fifteen and half.

Norman's death haunts me and his many friends half a century later.

On Thursday, September 17, 1959, Norman Schumacher died. Here's what I wrote in my diary that day:

"It's a great shock—he died of complications resulting in (sic) a football game when his kidney was ruptured...My friend died!!...I still have his glove and bat..."

And on Friday, September 18, I wrote..."His funeral was today. I went. Was a pall-bearer—took off from school. Many people went."

Ironically, Milwaukee was hit by a second tragedy the very next day, the Sabbath, Saturday, September 19—Mrs. Sylvia Fink was brutally shot to death.

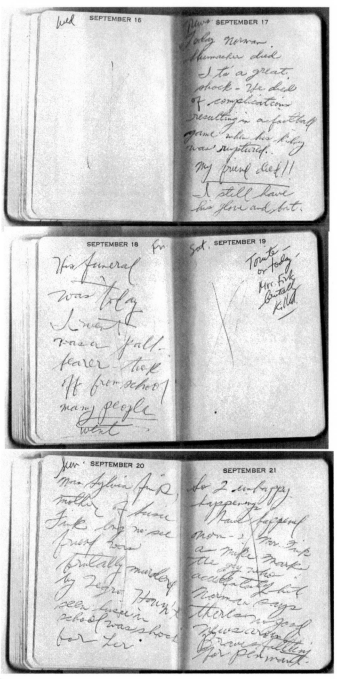

I end my diary on Sunday, September 20 with: "Mrs. Sylvia Fink, mother of Susie Fink long no see friend (sic) was brutally murdered by Negro....So 2 unhappy happenings have happened—Norm and Mrs. Fink. As Mike Marks, the guy who accidentally hit Norman (in the kidneys) says—there's no good news around... Braves also falling from pennant (race)...."

Monday, September 7, 1959, was my very first day at Washington High School. I was excited. Then the news hit us that Sabbath and a few days later.

On September 12, 1959, (the Jewish Sabbath), the guys stopped by my house to say they were going to play football after shul (synagogue). I was forbidden to play ball on the Sabbath, any kind of ball. My mom would not let me. I wonder to this day—did that "save" my life or at least minimize my guilt by not being there that fateful afternoon? So, Sol Lewin, Michael Marks, Shelly Bankier, and Normie Schumacher set out to play, none knowing that it would be Norman's last days on earth.

Norm was a special guy. He had a special charisma. I can still see his warm, somewhat tired, but lively eyes. He was talented, played trumpet, invented new games and kuntzim (stunts). Some of them were risky. I remember as kids we all would go out at night on mild summer evenings and peek into windows and startle people with strange noises. At times, we even saw people naked . It was erotic and exciting.

A naturally funny guy, a born leader, he was our leader in many ways.

The next day, Sunday, I heard that while playing tackle football (without padding), he was kicked in the kidney. We thought that Michael Marks kicked

95

him, but Sol said he didn't know who actually kicked him but that he was blamed. Maybe they were all blamed. To this day, no one knows who actually kicked him.

Norm continued to play even though he said he felt "bad." He went to Sol's house to wait for his parents, Sam and Rose Schumacher. They owned a small grocery store, Roosevelt Foods, on 14th and North Avenue, about thirty blocks from the football field, which was near Washington High School, at the corner of Sherman Boulevard and Center Street on the northwest side of Milwaukee. They walked about eight blacks from my house to get there.

Funny, I still remember so clearly the guys coming to my house and begging me to join them and my mom saying "No, not on the Sabbath". I watched them trudge down the street to the field.

But at eight o'clock that Saturday evening, the pain got much worse. Norm was rushed to Mt Sinai Hospital for an emergency operation. His kidney and surrounding tissue were destroyed and though he lingered for a few more days, they could not save him. He died September 17, 1959.

There were many rumors and questions about his death. Looking at his photos, one sees a somewhat pale young man. Perhaps, he had a pre-existing condition; some said he only had one working kidney. Others, that he caught pneumonia in the hospital or got an infection. I have not seen the hospital records, but I will one day. But if he had two working kidneys, he could have survived with only one. Today, he would have lived. Something, I believe, went wrong in the hospital.

Still, we were told that slow internal bleeding led to Norm's death. There were rumors of medical incompetence. His death is still a mystery.

Norman Schumacher in 1957 at his bar-mitzvah

Norman Schumacher

Rose & Sam Schumaker in their store in Milwaukee. (1940's - 1950-'s)

SOL LEWIN'S STORY

Sol was not only a great basketball player; he was an even better football player, a sport he loved even more than basketball. A great wide-receiver, he could have gone all pro like his friend Dennis Williamson who was drafted by the Cleveland Browns in 1967. But Sol was stopped from ever playing football again; but his natural ability at sports could not be contained so he put his energy into basketball.

It seemed that something died in Sol and in Michael Marks, and maybe in Sheldon and I as well, but to a lesser degree. Maybe as young kids, maybe we believed that we were in some way to blame fro Norman's death. Maybe less so for me, because miraculously, I was not allowed to play on the Sabbath for as the "Good Book" says: "Keep that day holy for I the Lord they God am Holy. Keep the Sabbath Day Holy, sayeth the Holy One, Blessed Be He."

Being Holocaust survivors, our parents did not know how to cope with death a second time. Coming to America, this death, so soon after the Shoah, was something they could not understand and in their fear, they blamed us "Amerikaner kids," us "wild American kids".

Years later, Sol would tell me, with much pain, that many blamed him for Norm's death. He felt better talking to me, forty years later, as if a great burden had been lifted. He was glad I called.

He also told me another "secret": his parents had lied to him about where he was born, and he was angry at them for that. It was a minor lie. They said Poland but a cousin told him it was actually Russia.

I told Sol that was common. My own passport says, for example, Austria even though I was actually born in Ukraine, USSR. Why the lies? Sol's parents, like mine, were not sophisticated people and rumors were rife in the DP camps about "Communism". The fear of being labeled a "Communist" was rampant in the 1950s. McCarthyism ruled the land; people were told to lie or else they would be sent back, that they would be unable to enter the "Promised Land" of America. So, they changed names, ages, birth dates, and places of birth.

Or, to hide other secrets, like earlier marriages and children.

Birth dates were changed to appear younger or older or maybe they just didn't know the exact English date, just the Hebrew one or "around Passover." For example, I was born "around Chanukah," the date set was December 2nd but it easily could have been the 15th or 21st. My friend Gershon Weissenberg, a talented raconteur, says I should have said the 25th, the day another Jew was born, but of course, I had no control over this, being so young.

Later, Sol lived with a non-Jewish woman, got into the healthcare field, and became isolated from the Jewish community, even from his old friends. However, today he lives in a beautiful home in Mequon, with a new wife, near a pool, with a shooting geyser. He seems content.

He works in the mobile nursing home business, a fitting business for a guy whose best friend died, perhaps unnecessarily, over fifty years ago.

MILT PIVAR'S STORY

I was fortunate to have met Milton (Milt) Pivar, the kind of man who is from my father's era, a kind of man you don't see much anymore. His name is well-known—Pivar Brothers Clothes, later he owned Goldman's Department Store on 10th and Mitchell. He remembers Guten's Deli and Elbaum's Bookstore on Center Street where they played poker games. He remembers Romenick the barber on Center Street and 50th. He remembers Garfinkel's "New Method Hebrew School" and Mordechai Melrood's more traditional Hebrew School. He went to Hi-Mount instead of Sherman Elementary School. He is also, ironically, the "last" of the Schumacher's, though he is not even a Schumacher, only married to one.

"They're all dead, Jack, all of them—the mother, the father and all of Norman's sisters and brothers."

Norman was the only offspring of Sam and Rose Schumacher. It was a big family, lots of Schumachers. Norman played trumpet"

But Norman had three siblings from an earlier marriage of his mother Rose to a Mr. Rossine—Carol

Pivar, Milt's wife; Marian (Larry) Plotkin, and Eugene Rossine, married to Nicki. All of them died young. Carol was 59; Marian, 68, and Eugene was in his early 60s.

"Yet Normie's parents, Rose and Sam, outlived all of them to a ripe old age. They had a grocery store, Roosevelt foods, on 14th and North, a Jewish area that turned black. Later they owned the McAlpin Hotel on Ocean Drive in Miami Beach." See photos.

"Yea, I remember the funeral. Rabbi Feldman officiated. You were right, Jack. Sam Schumacher nearly fell into the grave, shouting: 'Take me, God, not Norman.'

OTHER TRAGEDIES AND SCANDALS

Later, the early deaths of such childhood friends Jackie Wendorf, Barry Ellman, Butchie Steinrad, and others like Washington High School luminaries Ron Franzmeier, and Kenny Hirschbein all contributed to a sense that life was precious and should not be wasted.

There have been other scandals and tragedies in Milwaukee: a federation campaign director was caught stealing; even as far back as the early 50s, such stealing has occurred—a rabbi at the old Milwaukee Hebrew academy on Teutonia Avenue stole money and absconded to Canada in the early 1950s; some say that this was a factor in the demise of the school; later, Harry Goldberg was caught embezzling; R. Sandy Parsons, former principal of Hillel Academy, was caught defrauding SSI; there was the case of Buzz Cody, a janitor at a temple who claimed he was beaten by neo-Nazis, except that he did it himself; it is believed he committed suicide after he was exposed as a fraud; a drowning at Camp Interlaken; and the tragic killing of 15-year-old Nancy Radbil while riding her bike on Menominee River Parkway; but the one that effected me the most in recent times was the sudden death of Benjamin "Baki" Eiseman Muchin in January of 2005. Baki was the son of musician and teacher Marge Eiseman and *Jewish Chronicle* editor and writer Andy Muchin.

Andy and I were both asked to write a history of the Jews of Milwaukee around that time, and even though we had a good outline of what to cover and adequate funding, the project fell through due to the tragedy.

BAKI MUCHIN'S SUDDEN DEATH

Baki Muchin, another young kid, also died suddenly in 2005 from some unknown physical or medical cause. He was the son of a colleague and a possible co-author, Andy Muchin. I didn't know Baki well. We played ball in the alley behind their house in Shorewood. He was a great little athlete and a wonderful kid.

Baki was an extraordinary young boy of 12 when he died. The cause was mysterious—a sudden swelling of the brain tissue which was severe enough to have disrupted his breathing and heart. (See Amy Silvers article in the *Milwaukee Journal-Sentinel*, 2005). No cause of death was immediately known.

He grew up chasing his older twin brothers, Jonathan and Jacob, fifteen at the time. Jacob also had a serious illness, leukemia, but happily he recovered; and Baki had an even younger brother Zachary, 9, at the time.

All the boys had talent as ball players. I know. I'm a pretty good ball player myself and I was a junior varsity basketball player at Washington High School back in 1961. I noticed their talent. But Baki was special. He had a special talent for playing, a natural rhythm and style that one is born with. In many ways, it reminded me of Sol Lewin, the guy who accidentally hit Normie Schumacher in the kidneys in 1959. He too had this God-given fluidity—long arms and fingers, natural grace, and a powerful body.

His father Andy was quoted in the Silver article: "(Baki) was not a big guy, but he was very graceful, very coordinated, and very fast. He could throw a ball very fast at 2 years old. From the time he was 3, he would play—he could play—pickup games in soccer."

And he was only 12 years old when he died.

CONCLUSIONS: *WHAT CAN ONE SAY?*

I am glad I wrote these stories down. In another generation or so, they will be lost. Sadly, I don't have all the details, maybe I never will. In some cases, such as with Norm Schumacher, I tracked down the sole surviving member of his family who was at his funeral, his brother-in-law Milt Pivar. At times, as with Milt or with Sol Lewin, it seemed as if they had been waiting decades, even half a century, to talk to someone about it. These are painful events and even half a century is not enough time to erase the pain, but they were relieved to talk about things so far away in time.

The suicides of the rabbis and the murders were ironically the *least* controversial. The controversial was always about the survivors and their children: they were always the most sensitive, as if I was touching holy ground and they either wanted to "protect" the

107

memory of their parents or argue that I "over-gener-
alized" or   that I am bringing up subjects that should
remain buried; that they are simply too sensitive or
one-sided to write about.

The reaction to my lectures when I speak on these
is often contentious—one person will get up immediately and say I am wrong—he or she knows many sane
and normal second gen; while a moment later, another
person in the same audience will spring up and say—
Dr. Porter is 100% correct.

Furthermore, some of the most poignant encounters
usually after my lecture, comes when someone tells
me quietly that as a second generation person, he or
she is passing on this "syndrome" to his/her child or
children, and it frightens them. This is usually abuse
of some kind—either physical or sexual—and it is
very scary for them, but also they are so relieved that
someone like me has raised the issue and they finally
have someone to talk to. They often are reluctant to
give me their name or even e-mail but I sense that I
have helped them and in any case, they know how to
reach *me*.

Regarding the other issues, they are often grateful
someone remembered; history usually tries to sup-
press such acts as suicide, marital scandal, or sudden
deaths in most social histories of communities, specifi-
cally close-knit communities like the Jews.

Jonathan Sarna and Hasia Diner, eminent Jewish
historians, have deplored that attitude and say that
history should include everything—the good, the bad,
and the ugly—warts and all, all the while, of course,
protecting the identities of living people and the innocent whenever possible and not sensationalizing

the events. But every social history of every group has such tragic events and they must be told. Often, they are front page news, such as the Rabbi Weinberg suicide or the Sylvia Fink murder, so there is no avoiding them. All the above were in the Milwaukee papers, often on front page.

But as you can see, my book is much more than about survivor children; it is about all the "secrets" in a small community like Milwaukee. Some are "open secrets" splashed across the front pages; and some are closely held secrets that no one has heard before.

I am a writer; I have tried to be sensitive; I had to— these were and are my friends—but I also had to be true to myself as a writer and chronicler. The stories had to be told sooner or later. I'm glad I told them. It was an honor to do so.

SOURCES AND BIBLIOGRAPHY

There are many books and resources on adoption. I was most influenced by Adam Pertman and his book *Adoption Nation* and by the books of Betty Jean Lifton, *Lost and Found* and *Twice Born: Memoirs of an Adopted Daughter*. The situation is much better today in terms of openness yet very little has been written on post-Holocaust adoptions; see for example the following books and movies on adoption: *The Memory Keeper's Daughter* (about concealed adoption); Laurie Bembenek, *Woman on Trial*; E. Wayne Carp, *Family Matters: Secrecy and Disclosure in the History of Adoption*, 1998; Sherrie Eldridge, *20 Things Adoptive Parents Need to Succeed*, 2009, with a good up-to-date resource section; Christina Fisanick, *Issues in Adoption*, 2009; plus a fascinating book by John H. Maclean, *The Russian Adoption Book: How to Adopt from Russia, Ukraine, and other places in Eastern Europe*. If only Fay and Ayala were aware of such books back then.

Allen, Woody, *Mighty Aphrodite*, Miramax Films, 1995. A film about concealed adoption. Told in a humorous way. Mira Sorvino won an Oscar for best supporting actress in this film.

111

Block, Doug, *51 Birch Street*, HBO/Cinemax Documentaries, 2005, color, 88 minutes. Not about adoption but about family secrets. In the midst of filming his parents, Block's mother suddenly dies and his 83-year-old father marries his secretary three months later. A powerful yet subtle tale, interspersing diary entries, letters, and interviews. It shows how little we really know about our parents.

Emile Durkheim, *Suicide (Le Suicide): A Study in Sociology*, New York: The Free Press, 1897, translated and reprinted 1951.

Encyclopedia Judaica entries on "Adoption," "Suicide" and the "Holocaust," Jerusalem, Israel: Keter Publishing, 1971.

Epstein, Helen, *Children of the Holocaust: Conversations with Sons and Daughters of Survivors*, New York: G.P Putnam's Sons, 1979. An important yet dated book with very little on their "secrets."

Porter, Jack Nusan, "Is There a Survivor's Syndrome? Psychological and Socio-Political Implications" *Journal of Psychology and Judaism*, Vol. 6, No. 1, Fall/Winter1981, pp. 33-52. I found a second and even a third-generation "syndrome" yet little was done about it. Also reprinted in my *The Genocidal Mind*, 2006.

_____"Holocaust Suicides" in my The *Genocidal Mind*, Lanham, MD: University Press of America, 2006. It also appeared in Harry James Cargas's book, *Problems Unique to the Holocaust*, Louisville, KY: The University of Kentucky University Press, 1999, pp. 51-66. Also see the sources section after the article for more on suicide and Holocaust survivors.

Porter, Jack Nusan, Gerry Glazer, and Sandy Aronin, *Happy Days Revisited: Growing Up Jewish in Ike's America*, Newton, Mass.: The Spencer Press and Lightning Source, 2010. The "happy" side of growing up in Milwaukee.

The Milwaukee Journal and *The Milwaukee Sentinel* articles can be found in the Milwaukee Public Library. Other sources are the Milwaukee Historical Society and the Milwaukee Jewish Archives and Museum, Jay Hyland, chief archivist. Plus of course, the many articles and books on adoption, sudden death, suicide, and cognate issues.

INDEX

Milwaukee Memories

CPSIA information can be obtained at www.ICGtesting.com
Printed in the USA
BVOW011814071011

273112BV00002B/11/P